# 25 WAYS TO WORK FROM HOME

## Smart Business Models to Make Money Online

By Jen Ruiz

# 25 Ways to Work from Home

Smart Business Models to Make Money Online

Published by Jen on a Jet Plane
https://jenonajetplane.com/

© 2020 Jen on a Jet Plane
Cover: MercDesign

All rights reserved.

No part of this publication may be copied, stored in a retrieval system, reproduced or transmitted in any form by any means, electronical, mechanical, recording or otherwise, except in brief extracts for the purpose of review, and no part of this publication may be sold or hired, without permission from the publisher. For permissions contact:

jenruiz@jenonajetplane.com

While all attempts have been made to verify the information provided in this publication, neither the author nor the publisher assumes any responsibility for errors, omissions, or contrary interpretations of the subject matter herein.

# Table of Contents

| | |
|---|---|
| **Preface** | v |
| **Introduction** | 1 |
| **Chapter One: Steady(ish) Paychecks** | 9 |
| Strategy No. 1: Teach English Online | 9 |
| Strategy No. 2: Virtual Assistant | 13 |
| Strategy No. 3: Self-Publish Books | 17 |
| Strategy No. 4: Freelance Writing | 21 |
| Strategy No. 5: Video Editing | 24 |
| Strategy No. 6: Gig Economy | 27 |
| **Chapter Two: Entrepreneurial Route** | 31 |
| Strategy No. 7: Start a Podcast | 31 |
| Strategy No. 8: Monthly Subscription/Membership | 35 |
| Strategy No. 9: YouTube Channel | 40 |
| Strategy No. 10: E-Commerce | 43 |
| Strategy No. 11: Private Coaching | 46 |
| Strategy No. 12: Travel Planner or Guide | 50 |
| Strategy No. 13: Online Courses | 54 |
| **Chapter Three: Blog and Social Media** | 59 |
| Strategy No. 14: Affiliate Marketing | 59 |
| Strategy No. 15: Advertising Revenue | 63 |

Strategy No. 16: Summits — 66

Strategy No. 17: Sponsored Content — 70

**Chapter Four: Tech Skills Required** — **75**

Strategy No. 18: Buy and Sell Websites — 75

Strategy No. 19: Install and Customize WordPress Themes — 79

Strategy No. 20: Graphic Design — 81

Strategy No. 21: Create an App — 84

**Chapter Five: Existing Assets** — **89**

Strategy No. 22: Rent Your Property — 89

Strategy No. 23: Sell Your Photos — 92

Strategy No. 24: Sell Clothing and Accessories — 96

Strategy No. 25: Offer Professional Services — 100

**Bonus** — **105**

**About the Author** — **107**

# *Preface*

Working in your pajamas is the dream. At least, it was my dream back when I was an attorney wearing suits on a daily basis. The thought of setting my own schedule, waking up without an alarm clock and not having to force myself to pay attention in a meeting seemed like the definition of "making it."

The problem was, that dream wasn't attainable. I had $200k+ in student loan debt and $2,000+ of South Florida living expenses to pay every month. I'd previously dipped my toes into the world of online work with little to no success.

I'd make $.10/survey online, or $10 total selling my belongings only to find out later I still needed them and spending more money to replace them than what I netted in the first place.

Why was I hustling so hard as a lawyer? Being a professional didn't carry the benefits I'd been led to believe it would. Even when I worked at a private firm, my associate salary was far from six figures.

Healthcare was not always provided and even when it was, it barely covered routine checkups. At one point I decided to ask for a raise. I read every article online on how to do so, calculated my value and made the ask, ultimately getting a salary bump of $5,000.

It came out to less than $100 more per paycheck.

I didn't need an extra $100 a month. I needed a few hundred, or dare I say it, a few *thousand* dollars more a month to really make a difference.

I knew something had to change but I didn't know where to begin. After all, no one else was doing things any differently.

Then one day I came across a post in a Facebook group talking about teaching English online. The girl who posted it was in her early 20's and traveling the world while working remotely.

Meanwhile, I was approaching 30 and stuck in a windowless office with a "prestigious" job, barely making ends meet.

I thought, "Why not me?" and so I applied.

It wasn't my first time applying to teach online. I'd previously tried to work with a tutoring service but was denied. I didn't have any teaching experience but I had spent time working with children in a volunteer capacity so I emphasized that this time around. It was enough to get me through and I was hired in early February 2017.

That month, I hustled. I taught every single morning before going to work, from 6am to 8:30am. Instead of sleeping, I taught Saturday and Sunday mornings from 2am to 10am. I burned myself out and it wasn't sustainable but in that first month I made $1,126.

$1,126!! There are only 28 days in February. I worked 19 of them, teaching trial classes at half price since I didn't have regular students yet. Despite all this, I still made money. *Real money*. More money than I expected to make and more than I realized could be earned online.

It was incredible. Suddenly, I had a cushion. I had excess funds. Even better, I had a way of earning more anytime, from anywhere around the world.

I used that side gig to help fund my "year of adventure" where I set out to take 12 trips in 12 months before my 30th birthday while still working full-time. It was a whirlwind but I surpassed my goal, taking 20 trips in 12 months to destinations like Cuba, Iceland, Thailand and Greece.

I found such great deals on my trips, like a $22 roundtrip flight to San Francisco and $16 flight to Ecuador, that people kept asking me about my cheap flight secrets so I published a book called, "The Affordable Flight Guide: How To Find Cheap Flights and Travel the World on a Budget." It became a #1 Amazon bestseller in multiple categories and 2018 Reader's Favorite Award winner.

The monthly royalties from my book, coupled with my teacher earnings, made me think I could actually make a go of remote work. That's when I did something crazy and quit my attorney job to travel and write full-time.

At the time, those were my only two income streams – teaching online and book royalties from Amazon. I had a website that I'd been running for more than 2 years but wasn't monetizing properly. I wouldn't necessarily advise others to take a big leap at that stage but I did was right for me.

Today, I have 8 different online income streams and am in the process of launching several others.

The biggest thing that has changed is my mindset. Now that I'm part of the digital entrepreneur community, I am surrounded by others who are thriving in their online businesses.

I'm not talking $1,126 either – I'm talking million dollar course launches, six-figure summits and 5-figure coaching clients. Knowing people who get paid well for their work has made me see that it's not only possible to step outside of the rat race – it's preferable.

You live a better life, with the freedom to manage your time and commitments. You have more financial security, in many cases making money while you sleep. You feel more fulfilled because you're following your purpose versus being a warm body in a seat at an office. You're engaged and tuned in and excited to wake up every morning.

One year after quitting my job, my remote work earnings surpassed my full-time attorney income. I now make more money as a travel blogger and writer than I did as an attorney.

As I write my 4$^{th}$ book while in pajamas, I can officially say I'm living the dream.

You don't need to waste years of your life trying to figure out what works.

You can make money online *easily* and *legitimately* using the methods I outline in this book. If it made it in the book, it's only because it's a monetization method I use myself or have seen work for someone I personally know.

Each chapter will outline a different type of remote work and has the basics you need to get started, from useful websites to real-life examples of others who've done it successfully. No job is perfect so I include some potential downsides and, conversely, when you know you "made it."

Note, you do _not_ need to have a degree to work from home. Many of the jobs outlined in this book, from starting an e-commerce store to freelancing, are open to people of all educational backgrounds and ages.

As a thank you for reading, I put together a private, limited-episode podcast called the "Work from Home Diaries," featuring interviews with real-life people who are making a living remotely. You'll find the link and password at the end of this book. With it, you'll have access to 4 hours of bonus content that will show you how easy it is for everyday people to transition to remote work.

Get your pajamas ready cause it's time to start monetizing your talents from home. Here's how to start making money online!

# Introduction

# 5 Pillars to Success in Remote Work

*"You wouldn't have the dream if you didn't already have what it takes within you to make it happen." – Marie Forleo*

Making a full-time living remotely is exponentially easier when you follow the five pillars of success. A pillar is a heavy support column that holds up a structure. Without them, you can still build a house. It just won't be sturdy. A strong gust of wind could come and knock it over at any time in the form of an economic recession, algorithm update or closure of a popular site or platform.

This is why for so many people, working remotely feels unstable. The good news it, it doesn't have to be that way. Here are 5 things successful remote workers value above all else.

### #1: Diversify Your Income Streams

The first and most important pillar to success is having multiple income streams. Everything online is fluid. Websites come and go. Traffic and demand for products wane seasonally. Technical issues could happen at any time.

If you're only making money one way and that income

stream runs out, you are going to kick yourself for thinking remote work was legitimate and go back to a more secure but unfulfilling position. The best way to ensure success as a remote worker is to have 5 or more equivalent income streams. That way, even if one of them is completely wiped out you can still keep moving forward with 80% of your expected earnings.

When you're thinking about diversification, try to span across different fields, categories and genres. For instance, if you're into fitness and wellness and have online courses and a workout subscription program, you might also want to consider directing your customers to a separate healthy eating blog with videos and recipes that you create. That way if anything were to happen where you can't physically workout, like an injury or complicated pregnancy, you would still have money coming in from the nutrition side of your business.

Moreover, that separate healthy recipe blog could attract new customers that were just looking to make dinner but could become fitness clients in the future.

### #2: Provide Free Value

A teacher in a leadership seminar once told me, "everyone is tuned in to W-I-I-F-M: What's in it for me?"

That's a phrase I constantly think about as an entrepreneur and digital creative. What are people getting out of the work that I'm doing? How am I adding value to their lives?

When you can figure out the answer to that question you will magically go from chasing and hounding down people to support you to having people flooding your inbox asking for your help.

People who provide value will always be in business. The format in which you deliver that value may change but the demand will remain.

It may seem counterintuitive but you will make more money when you give away some of your best content for free. By providing value from the get-go through your lead magnets and introductory webinars, you're more likely to hook a customer and keep them coming back. If you give them something they need, the sale will be made for you. If you sell without ever giving value first, no one is going to have a reason to buy.

Make sure you're clear on what you're providing, how it's different from the competition and what's in it for the customers that you want to attract. Then flood them with free content. The reality is no one will consume every single thing you're creating (except your mom) so you don't have to worry that by giving away free content they won't have a need for your paid product.

Even a client who follows you religiously would still be likely to buy a related product, such as a course, webinar or book, for the convenience of having all the information in one place.

Don't be afraid to give away free value. The more you help people without asking for anything in return, the more likely they'll be to invest in your services and work with you in the future.

## #3: Build an Email List

The biggest mistake I see entrepreneurs and remote workers do is wait to build their email list. They think, "oh I'm not selling a product," or "I don't have anything to say."

Let me put it to you this way. In the past, people used to spend their workdays going door-to-door to reach potential customers. Heck, it is still used today as valid strategy for political staffers wanting to collect votes – of the elderly population.

If you want to reach anyone 40 or under, you go through their email address.

Imagine what those traveling salesmen of the 1950's would say if they knew there was a way to get their message before hundreds, thousands, even millions of people all at the click of a button? That instead of having to walk to 100 houses in a day, you could reach a hundred people in a minute.

Emails are our virtual houses. They're our personal space online where we allow others to visit by invitation only. They can't show up unannounced or our guard dog, the spam filter, takes care of them.

Email addresses are so valuable that companies actually pay to collect them. They shell out $15,000 in Facebook ads like nothing in the hopes of getting a few hundred email addresses.

If you have an invested audience or clientele, no matter how small, you need to collect their email addresses. If you have a website, social media platform or online store and you're letting people just come, browse and leave without even presenting them with the opportunity to subscribe to your list, you're losing out on future business.

Every day you don't have an email list is a day you're bleeding warm leads. You're letting people who have shown an interest in you, your services or your product leave into the depths of the internet, never to be heard from again.

I cannot emphasize this enough. If you have 100k followers on Instagram but no way to reach them outside of the platform, you do not own that audience. You cannot count on that readership or clientele. If Instagram decides to delete your account, you get hacked or if the platform goes away altogether, so do your followers.

I do recommend emailing your list consistently but it does not have to be frequently. It could be once a month, quarterly – the important thing is to pick a schedule that you can stick to.

As for what to say, think of it like writing a letter to your friends. Send life updates, tips, relevant content. Provide *value* in your area of expertise.

I could write an entire book on email marketing but suffice it to say this is a pillar for a reason so stop fighting it and just embrace it.

## #4: Don't Let the Haters Deter You

A friend once told me, "Jen, it doesn't matter if you're the juiciest peach on the tree. There will still be someone who doesn't like peaches." The sentiment was so sweet I didn't have the heart to tell her it was me – I don't like peaches. Even the smell of them makes me sick. Fruit preferences aside, however, the message got across. You can't please everybody and this holds doubly true online.

The internet is going to be your workplace now. You might get disheartened the first time someone leaves you a bad review or writes a nasty comment. You might even start to question why you're doing it at all. Just know that every second you spend focusing on haters is a second you could have devoted to an online community that supports and uplifts you.

Haters point out other people's flaws while sitting on the sidelines – they're too afraid to even play the game. This is especially the case for internet trolls who have anonymity and the distance of a screen to embolden them.

Do not let one angry or dissatisfied person on the internet (there will be many over the course of a long and successful digital career) stop you from putting yourself out there.

## #5: Done is Better than Perfect

Perfectionism and imposter syndrome go hand in hand and they both result in one thing –thinking of great ideas but never actually executing them. Let's address both right now.

Perfect is an impossible standard to meet. If that's what you're aiming for, let us know when you achieve Android status, they might be casting for the new Star Trek. We mere humans, however, know that we **will** mess up. It **will** happen. It's not a matter of "if" but "when."

The funny thing is messing up doesn't matter nearly as much as how you respond and act to remedy your mistakes. Instead of sitting on your manuscript or refusing to venture out as a designer because you fear that you're not ready, you might mess up or your work is imperfect, toss those limiting thoughts aside. Understand that excellence is attained by action and refinement along the way. No one starts at 100%, not even Beyonce.

As for imposter syndrome, you may be thinking, "who am I to start this podcast/YouTube Channel/blog? No one will actually listen to me. There are people out there who know way more about this than I do." Again, this is the wrong standard. The question is not whether you are the world's foremost expert on a topic. The question is whether you know more than the person you're looking to help and have something of value to offer. Bobby Flay (or insert your favorite chef here) might be the world's best cook but if 6 billion people had to line up to learn from him and him alone we'd all be in trouble.

There's room for you in whatever space you're looking to enter. Don't let imposter syndrome stop you from sharing your gifts with the world.

# CHAPTER ONE

# Steady(ish) Paychecks

*"I could either watch it happen or be part of it." –
Elon Musk*

### Strategy No. 1: Teach English Online

Teaching English online is one of the steadiest options out there in terms of payment and is a good steppingstone for anyone skeptical about online work.

If you're from the United States it's easy to find a job teaching English since most language learners want to speak with an American accent. British, South African, New Zealand or Australian citizens would have a harder time finding work.

You're not limited to language education, however. You can teach any subject online so long as you have the expertise and clientele. You don't need teaching experience or certifications, although having either one will put you a step ahead of other applicants.

**PAY RATE:**

Online English teachers make $16-$20/hour on average.

**WHO IT'S SUITED FOR:**

If you like children and flexibility, this is a good gig for you. There's also work available teaching adults online but those jobs are less common and not as lucrative.

You need to be engaging enough to hold the attention of a child over video. Ideally, you're someone who is patient, speaks with their hands and has a lot of energy at off-peak hours like early morning or late night. You're also perky generally and like to smile a lot.

**SUCCESS STORIES:**

I have been teaching English online to Chinese children in my spare time since February 2017. I work with VIPKid and consistently make $1,000+/month with 2-3 hours of my time a day.

Malia Yoshioka, a blogger a Shoyu Sugar, works full-time as an online teacher in various subjects, platforms and to students of all ages. She makes a living primarily from teaching and is able to set her own schedule while living abroad.

**HELPFUL WEBSITES:**

There are more than 60 websites where you can teach online. Here are 5 of the highest paying companies that you should consider:

1) VIPKID (https://www.vipkid.com)

Ranked the #1 Company for remote work by Forbes in 2018, VIPKid is among the highest paying online teaching jobs you can get. The job requires teaching English to students living in China who are between 5 to 12 years old. Contract rates are capped at $22/hour but you can make up to $24/hour with bonuses by showing up on time and teaching more than 45 classes a month.

Classes are one-on-one and last 25 minutes each. Teaching contracts last 6 months and there's no minimum number of classes you need to teach. You need a bachelor's degree and American accent to qualify. You do not need a TEFL certification but they have a VIPKid TEFL Program you can elect to complete free of charge.

2) Magic Ears (https://t.mmears.com)

Magic Ears is based in Beijing and involves teaching English to children in China ages 5-12. Classes are also 25 minutes long and pay a base rate of $9-$11 per class. If you teach more than 60 classes a month during peak hours and start at the highest pay level you can make up to $26 an hour. Lessons are 4-on-1 and like VIPKid, you need a bachelor's degree and American accent to continue.

3) Two Sigmas (https://www.twosigmas.com)

Two Sigmas serves as an intermediary connecting you with online teaching schools. They require a bachelor's degree and TEFL certification. The pay, length of classes, length of contract and age of the students will vary depending on the school you work with. The average salary is $20/hour.

4) italki (https://www.italki.com)

This site promotes learning of all languages for all ages. If you speak another language or have an accent that is not American, you can apply here. To be selected as a "community tutor," you must show you're at least a native speaker in the language you're seeking to teach. There's also the higher certification of "professional teacher" that requires you to submit proof of training.

Teachers set their own rates and determine the length of classes. The average rate is $10 an hour, of which italki takes 15%. That means a community tutor can expect to make approximately $17/hour.

5) DadaABC (https://dadaabc.com)

This company is based out of Shanghai and teaches to students ages 4-16. Classes are a half hour or hour long and contracts last 6 months or a year. You need a bachelor's degree and to be a native English speaker. Payment ranges from $15-$25/hour and the average teacher makes $17/hour.

**THE DOWNSIDE:**

Since most classes are for students based out of Asia, you might have to wake up early or teach late at night. It can also be difficult to get a raise and the cancellation policies are inflexible, favoring the student and not the teacher.

**YOU KNOW YOU MADE IT WHEN…**

You're a highly rated, in-demand teacher. You open up a time slot and it fills up immediately. You have a roster of students that are a delight to work with and blend well with your teaching style.

You set your own hours, likely during the morning or at night, and have the bulk of your day to devote to other projects or daily tasks. When you travel, you don't have to miss out on money. You can open up as many or as few time slots as you want and teach from anywhere around the world.

You work 120 hours a month and make $2,880 with the occasional $5 gift card or bonus thrown in. Someone else handles the business aspect, recruiting clients and putting together your lesson plans. You just show up and talk.

## Strategy No. 2: Virtual Assistant

One of the first jobs people think about when they think about remote work is offering virtual assistant ("VA") services.

A virtual assistant is just like it sounds — it's a person who takes care of tasks online that have become too menial or tedious for others to do themselves. They're just like a regular assistant, only instead of picking up your dry cleaning they answer emails or handle your social media accounts.

**PAY RATE:**

Varies widely depending on the services offered but one client can range from $300-$500/month on average for part-time hours. This amount more than doubles for corporate clients.

**WHO IT'S SUITED FOR:**

If you like being the person behind the scenes, are organized and able to manage multiple tasks at once then this is the gig for you. You don't mind doing grunt work or tedious tasks. You are timely and can deliver on a deadline.

**SUCCESS STORIES:**

A great example and resource in this field is Hannah from Digital Nomad Kit. Hannah started off as a VA and after 10 years of travel is now an expert in freelancing. She helps entrepreneurs launch, manage and curate remote teams and offers private coaching and consulting. She has a free 5-day VA challenge on her website as well as resources to help you get started.

Another example is Sierra from Sierra Virtual Solutions. Sierra is a blogger who monetized her existing skills by offering her expertise to others. You can see her rates and packages on the website to get a better idea of how to structure your pricing.

**HELPFUL WEBSITES:**

1) Boldly (www.boldly.com)

Boldly is a company that provides a range of fully remote services for business based in North America and Europe. They hire virtual assistances as employees to perform a range of tasks for their clients. Applicants must have at least 7 years of experience in their field of expertise and can expect to make between $37-$43/hour.

2) We Are Virtual Assistants (https://www.wearevirtualassistants.com)

Formed by a founder of Boldly, We Are Virtual Assistants is a site meant to give you all the tools you need to launch your VA business. They also have job listings in areas such as marketing, social media and project management.

3) BELAY (www.belaysolutions.com)

BELAY is a company that hires VA's at an hourly rate for their clients. VA's can expect to earn $16-$20 an hour. They have a difficult vetting and interview process and require at least 5 years of experience in an administrative role. They guarantee a robust support staff and steady work if accepted.

4) Zirtual (www.zirtual.com)

Zirtual provides VA's for entrepreneurs, professionals and small teams. They have remote virtual assistant positions throughout North America with working hours of 9am to 6pm. You only need one year of experience and can make anywhere from $28-$33/hour.

5) Time Etc. (www.web.timeetc.com)

Time Etc. is another virtual workplace platform with hundreds of freelancers in their employ. They will market your specific skill set; you just need 5 years of experience. They offer a fixed rate of $22-$26/hour depending on your area of expertise.

6) Your Virtual Assistant BFF (https://www.facebook.com/groups/yourVABFF)

This is one of several FB groups aimed at fostering a VA community. I like that they frequently post job listings and engaging content. The search button in these groups comes in handy when you have a specific question you can't find the answer to anywhere else.

**THE DOWNSIDE:**

When you're starting out, it can be hard to find clients. Your services might also be looked at as expendable if your clients ever need to make budget cuts. Depending on the services offered, you could be doing mundane or repetitive work.

**YOU KNOW YOU MADE IT WHEN...**

Being employed as a VA is good money and for many, just being able to make a living in the field is enough.

For those with more ambitious goals, starting your own VA business could be very lucrative.

Let's say you're a whiz at Pinterest and want to start your own Pinterest VA service. You have one or two accounts you manage with good engagement and have a portfolio of existing content you can showcase to potential clients, from collage to video pins.

You can charge $300+ a month to create, post and promote 20 pins per month per client, including optimized descriptions and hashtags and requesting to join 8 new group boards per month. If you get 10 clients, that's $3,000/month for 200 pins. If each pin takes you 10-20 minutes and each group board request takes you 1-2 minutes, that's 40-70 hours of work a month to make a full-time income.

If you get corporate clients, you can more than triple your rates and decrease your work. A franchise or small business could pay anywhere from $1k-$5k/month for social media management depending on the depth of your services.

To get new clients, you offer referral fees to your existing clients. To retain your clients, you offer a loyalty bonus every year or grandfather them in by offering a set rate in perpetuity.

Now, you as the owner of Awesome Pinterest Firm get to work from home. Depending on the demand and number of clients you can scale your company to hire your own employees, incorporate as a business entity to reap the tax benefits and make upwards of 6 figures as a digital entrepreneur.

## Strategy No. 3: Self-Publish Books

Self-publishing books online is easier than ever thanks to Amazon. They own 80% of the e-book market and have minimal barriers to entry. Authors can write a book one time and reap passive income for years by selling more of that same product and related services.

Even if you don't like writing, you can curate a collection of stories (think Chicken Soup for the Soul), interviews, information guides (like Frommer's) or hire a ghostwriter.

**PAY RATE:**

Amazon's publisher program (unlike its affiliate program) is one of the steadiest paychecks of the online world. They pay monthly and you can earn 70% commission on books priced between $2.99 and $9.00. The amount of money you make will depend on how many books you sell, your genre, how many other books you've written and the price. A self-published author can make anywhere from $500-$1,000/month with their first or second book. Crossing $1,000/month is an important author milestone.

**WHO IT'S SUITED FOR:**

A fondness for writing is ideal but not necessary for the reasons stated above. You should have an interest in digital marketing and e-commerce.

Ideally, anyone looking to self-publish will have what's called an "author platform," a.k.a a minimum of 1,000 email subscribers, private group members or similarly invested readers ready to buy your book when it come out. If you don't have that currently, start building it before you publish your book.

**SUCCESS STORIES:**

Amanda Hocking is among the highest grossing self-published authors of all times, selling millions of young adult books without an agent or publishing house and starting a bidding war between Amazon and the "big 5" publishers before ultimately landing at St. Martin's press.

Joanna Penn is a New York Times and USA Today bestselling self-published author of 30+ fiction and nonfiction books. She also runs a website called The Creative Penn, a valuable resource for hopeful authors.

**HELPFUL WEBSITES:**

1) Kindlepreneur (www.kindlepreneur.com)

This site is run by Dave Chesson and has an accompanying podcast, post of which are a wealth of information when it comes to publishing books. There is a free Amazon ads course you can take to learn more about the algorithm. There's also the Kindlepreneur Calculator, a free and unique tool that translates

Amazon rankings into an estimated number of book sales per day so you can calculate how much your competitors are earning from their book sales.

2) 99Designs (www.99designs.com)

Your book cover is the single most important tool in your sales arsenal – make it count. You want your topic to be immediately discernible, your text to be legible and the design to look professional. Instead of describing what you want to one specific designer and hoping they get it right, I recommend using 99 Designs to have professional artists prepare and submit their ideas to you based on your project specifications, giving you 30 or more options to choose from.

3) Bargain Booksy (www.bargainbooksy.com)

There are dozens of bok promotion sites out there but more often than not they don't yield a return on investment. If you're going to promote your book, Bargain Booksy and its sister site FreeBooksy provide an affordable email blast service that will result in actual book sales and profits.

4) Adazing (www.adazing.com)

Adazing is a website that I first found when looking for free mockups (3D images of your book cover to use for promotion). I am now a part of "The Author Lab," a great resource for anyone looking to do most of the work themselves and on a budget. It includes book cover designs, chapter formatting, customizable GIF's and more.

5) N.Y. Book Editors (www.nybookeditors.com/blog)

No matter your genre, New York Book Editors will have helpful tips and advice. I'm on their email list and am a frequent reader of the blog. They also offer editing and critique services but I've only used them for their content so far.

**THE DOWNSIDE:**

To be profitable as an author, you need to keep writing. Most authors making six figures or more have 20 or more published books. Think of the famous authors you know like Stephen King or Nora Roberts – they don't just have one book. It can also be a solitary lifestyle as you need to be left alone for hours at a time to write.

**YOU KNOW YOU MADE IT WHEN...**

You're an author with more than a dozen books and a dedicated readership. You make $5,000-$10,000/month in passive income from your book collection. You use your books as a lead magnet to gain more customers and sell higher ticket products, like courses and coaching.

You are regarded as an expert in your field because you are an author and are able to use your status to land speaking engagements, book signings and TV interviews. You've won awards for your writing, either fiction or nonfiction, and your books are so popular there's a waiting list to borrow them at the library.

You spend your days writing, marketing existing books and coming up with products to offer as upsells for those who enjoy your writing.

## Strategy No. 4: Freelance Writing

Nowadays traditional journalism outlets are relying more on freelancers than staffers for their articles. This is a broad category that can encompass everything from copywriting to ghostwriting. Writers with a special niche i.e. writing "About Me" pages or Facebook ad copy, are all in demand.

**PAY RATE:**

Beginner writers can expect to make $.10 - $.25/word. Intermediate writers make anywhere between $.25 and $.50/word. Experienced and award-winning writers can make more than $1.00/word. Articles typically range from 600-3,000 words depending on the topic and platform.

**WHO IT'S SUITED FOR:**

Unlike book publishing, you need to enjoy writing to be a freelance writer. You should also be prolific and able to work well under deadlines.

If you want to work for a major publication versus, say, a dental office that wants you to write content for their website, you'll need to keep abreast of breaking news and be addicted to Twitter. You should also have a lot of resiliency and not take rejection personally.

**SUCCESS STORIES:**

Lola Ann Mendez is a successful freelance travel journalist and has been featured by major publications such as CNN, Lonely Planet and Cosmopolitan.

Travis Levius is also a successful freelance travel writer with bylines in National Geographic and Forbes. He offers a travel writing coaching program with one-on-one sessions for anyone looking to break into the field.

**HELPFUL WEBSITES:**

1) Dream of Travel Writing (www.dreamoftravelwriting.com)

Run by Gabi Logan, Dream of Travel Writing is a blog and resource for those wanting to get published in large magazines and print publications. She has a "Travel Magazine Database" accessible by subscription only that has information on all the major outlets, include the contact information of the editor you need to reach and summary of the magazine's sections so you can craft a relevant pitch. She also offers one-on-one coaching sessions and in-person writing retreats.

2) The Write Life (www.thewritelife.com)

This website focuses on all things writing, from publishing to starting your own blog. Check out their extensive freelancing section for tips, how-to guides and inspiration. If you're not sure where to start check out this post on where to find freelance writing jobs.

3) Twitter (www.twitter.com)

Believe it or not, Twitter is a valuable tool for finding writing gigs. Search by hashtags for terms like "journo request" or "writers wanted." You can also follow the editors of magazines you want to write for so you get familiar with the content they're publishing and are the first to know when they put out a call for submissions. You can also follow accounts for job boards specifically like @write_jobs and @whopayswriters.

4) Binder Groups on Facebook

In the wake of the infamous "binders full of women" comment, "binders" has actually become a unifying term for females and minorities alike. There are several groups on Facebook with the word in its title where you can connect with other writers and find pitching opportunities. I suggest starting with "Binders Full of Editors Seeking Their Freelance Writers and Vice Versa."

5) Make a Living Writing (www.makealivingwriting.com)

This website is meant to be a catch-all resource for freelancers. You can find writing contests, pitch templates, mentoring and a library of blog posts aimed to help you navigate the freelance world at all stages of interest, from beginner to mid-career writer.

**THE DOWNSIDE:**

You may have to chase down your paycheck from time to time, or deal with delays in payment. If a website or brand you're writing for goes out of business, you may even need to resort to legal action to get paid.

**YOU KNOW YOU MADE IT WHEN:**

You write for major publications like the New York Times and The Washington Post. People are so moved by your words that you're frequently contacted after publishing a piece – 90% fans, 10% trolls.

You never get tired of seeing your name in print and frequently go on press trips, reviewing a local restaurant or writing about a new summer concert series. You get sweet

VIP passes and comps wherever you go. When you write for private clients, you're able to charge high rates because of your credentials.

You could write 3-5 new articles a month -- actually enjoying the process of researching and putting them together -- and make $5,000.

Alternatively, you could have private clients on retainer, drafting email newsletters or social media posts as needed and making $6,000/month with 2-3 corporate clients.

## Strategy No. 5: Video Editing

If you're skilled with a camera, video editing is a field that's going to grow rapidly in the coming years. Most brands are skewing towards video now, adding clips to all-text articles online an focusing on video-based social media channels like TikTok and YouTube.

**PAY RATE:**

Professional video editors can make between $75-$150/hour or bill a flat rate per service, i.e. $2,000 for a 10-minute video. Typically, it takes a minimum of 5 hours to professionally edit 2 minutes of video. Rates will be commensurate with experience, equipment and skills offered, such as drone footage or special effects.

**WHO IT'S SUITED FOR:**

You like to be behind the camera, not in front of it. You have the ability to hyper focus and spend hours in front of a screen playing with the timing of clips down to the second.

You're an A/V nerd at heart and get excited about new camera equipment. In the event of a fire, you would request that firefighters save your tech tools first, pictures later.

**SUCCESS STORIES:**

On a large scale, companies like Salt and Lime media do video production, which includes casting and filming, for major corporations like Facebook. These are 6-figure contracts. If you only want to focus on post-production, you can offer your services to brands like this or start your own small editing company.

Another example is Juliana Broste, an award-winning videographer and host at Traveling Jules who offers video editing services as part of her portfolio.

**HELPFUL WEBSITES:**

1) Animoto (www.animoto.com)

This is a video editing program that's great for beginners. There are done-for-you templates and a library of stock photos and videos you can use without worrying about licensing. It's a subscription-based model with plans starting at $8/month when paid yearly. I recommend purchasing on Black Friday if you can since they always have a big sale.

2) Adobe Premier Pro (www.adobe.com)

This is part of the Adobe Creative Suite and is an investment ranging from $20-$50+/month depending on how many apps you want to purchase. If you're serious about pursuing this as a full-time job you should invest in the full package which also includes valuable photo editing tools like Photoshop that you'll need when making thumbnail covers.

3) Camtasia (www.camtasia.com)

In contrast to Adobe's monthly (and never-ending) subscription model, Camtasia is a one-time payment of $250 and is one of the best editing platforms on the market. You can easily compose video, narrate, add subtitles, share your screen and add special effects. It's an upgrade from iMovie.

4) DIY Video Editor Blog (www.diyvideoeditor.com)

This website is dedicated to helping new at-home film makers and editors succeed. You'll find helpful quick start guides, tutorials, software reviews and industry news here.

5) Film Editing Pro (www.filmeditingpro.com)

For those wanting to take their video editing skills to the next level, this site has training courses dedicated to specific projects and programs like the art of trailer editing and an Adobe Premier Pro tutorial. They have a focus on editing for Hollywood projects, like feature films and commercials.

**DOWNSIDE:**

It can take hours to edit just a few minutes of video, even for the most experienced editor. Also, the equipment and software can be expensive. There are ways to start for free but it will require a sizeable investment of money and time to do this as a full-time job.

**YOU KNOW YOU MADE IT WHEN:**

You have a video editing and production company that regularly books 5 and 6-figure projects with brands and individuals. You are regarded as an industry leader and are a whiz at your chosen video editing platform.

You have the reputation and discretion to choose which projects you take on. You work in a field that excites you, like editing movie trailers or luxury vacation promos. You have the option to scale your business into a full production company, take on projects as you see fit or and land major contracts with companies like Twitter and Disney.

## Strategy No. 6: Gig Economy

This category encompasses jobs in many different fields but I'm grouping it all together under the umbrella of "gig economy" since apps like Uber and Instacart are redefining the way we do business.

By definition, the gig economy is a labor market characterized by short-term contracts or freelance work as opposed to permanent jobs. For our purposes, we're going to focus on work you can do from home instead of delivery apps and the like.

In the beginning, pick one platform and stick to it. Resist the urge to branch out and be everywhere because that means your reviews will be scattered as well, never allowing you to really stand out and excel in any one place.

**PAY RATE:**

This will vary depending on the kind of job you do. Generally, the gig economy pays you for the task, not by the hour, so you need to be careful how you set your rates or what jobs you accept. It may seem tempting to ghostwrite a blog post for $50 but if it ends up taking you 8 hours it's hardly worth your time.

Fees can range from $5 to $1,000+ per task or project, with rates becoming higher for anyone with experience or special skills.

**WHO IT'S SUITED FOR:**

Getting your start through the gig economy is great for someone you're looking to test the waters. Maybe you're not sure what you're an expert in yet and just want to try out general tasks. You can find work on these sites doing anything from driving to putting together someone's Tinder profile.

If you're a jack of all trades, you'll do well in this arena. You will also need to be persistent about pitching and landing jobs and make a good enough impression when you get hired to merit rave reviews since those will be important for your bottom line.

**SUCCESS STORIES:**

Alex Fasulo has a 6-figure freelance business on Fiverr. She offers writing, editing and photography services and has a blog and courses to help you do the same. She's been featured by Entrepreneur Magazine, Forbes and Yahoo Finance for her success as a pro member of the popular freelancing site.

**HELPFUL WEBSITES**

1) Fiverr (www.fiverr.com)

Fiverr began under the premise the small gigs could be done for $5. It's since evolved past that and most freelancers offer their services for significantly more but you'll still find a clientele that is looking to pay the last possible for the best results.

2) Upwork (www.upwork.com)

Upwork is to Fiverr what Target is to Walmart. The main difference is that on Fiverr you set up a profile and post your rates and interested parties reach out to you. On Upwork, you bid on jobs that suit your qualifications.

3) Freelancer (www.freelancer.com)

Freelancer is an Australian company that works similarly to Upwork -- they have a competitive bidding process where you apply for jobs among many other candidates. They also hold competitions and offer cash prizes. While the jobs are the same the pay rates tend to be lower here, as are the expectations regarding quality of work.

4) PeoplePerHour (www.peopleperhour.com)

This is a UK-based platform that is aimed at a European market. They have a bid process for jobs but also allow freelancers to post "hourlies," set packages that clients can independently find and purchase based on their needs like Fiverr.

5) TopTal (www.toptal.com)

Of all the websites listed, this is the most exclusive. They have rigorous acceptance standards and focus on staffing freelance software developers, finance experts, designers and product managers.

**DOWNSIDE:**

I caution you against using the gig economy as a long-term strategy. The sites I mention are a great starting point but as you grow to develop your skills and portfolio you'll find there's a lot of competition, low pay rates, poor employee policies and high payouts just for using their platform.

**YOU KNOW YOU MADE IT WHEN:**

I would say you know you made it when you no longer have to rely on the gig economy for work. However, strictly by the standards of these freelancing sites, you can say you made it when your profile receives a special badge or acknowledgement, you're in demand as a freelancer and you have to turn away orders because you have more orders than you can fill.

You can charge premium rates because you have a track record of delivering quality content and your reviews show that to potential customers. You're at the top of the freelancing pool and instead of bidding for jobs, jobs come to you.

# CHAPTER TWO

# *Entrepreneurial Route*

*"All our dreams can come true, if we have the courage to pursue them."*
*– Walt Disney*

### Strategy No. 7: Start a Podcast

Podcasting began around 2004 and since then has grown exponentially. As radio gets phased out, podcasts are in. They can be stopped, rewound and replayed on demand. They can teach us important skills and entertain us. Best of all, they're accessible anytime from our mobile devices, so we don't need to be in a car or have internet service to listen to them.

It's not hard to see why podcasts are catching on. If you're already an avid listener, perhaps starting one should be the next move for you.

**PAY RATE:**

The industry standard for advertising rates is anywhere from $15-$25 for 10-60 seconds per 1,000 listeners. This means that with 5,000 listeners you could bring in $125 in exchange for 60 seconds of airtime. You can also promote related products through affiliate links. If you talk about business, for instance, you could link to a particular software program in your show notes and get paid for anyone that signs up through your link.

I will note that this is not the most lucrative avenue if you're seeking to *only* monetize a podcast. A podcast is tool to get in front of a larger audience and direct them to more profitable income streams. Many podcasters will tell you they don't make much money off their podcast and do it because they love it. Done right, it can be the key to success and distinguisher that sets you apart from your competitors.

**WHO IT'S SUITED FOR:**

A lot of podcasters have a background in the radio industry but that's certainly not a requirement. Same goes for having a smooth or soothing voice – it's a bonus but it's not like you're narrating Planet Earth so don't let it hold you back if your voice is high-pitched or you have a weird laugh (like me!).

The hosts who do well typically offer value in one of four ways: 1) interview experts in their field; 2) give tips and how-to's for listeners; 3) provide entertainment in the form of a story, or; 4) answer audience questions.

Generally, a successful podcaster has a fondness for tech and gadgets. They are always carrying around a portable mic and care a lot about sound quality. Again, this is a trait that can be learned as you develop your craft and not a prerequisite for entry.

**SUCCESS STORIES:**

John Lee Dumas from Entrepreneurs on Fire was one of the original podcasters and an example of how a podcast can be the base of a 7-figure business. John distinguished himself from others by starting early in the game and doing a podcast daily at a time when his competitors were only airing a new show once or twice a week.

He's now the owner of Fire Nation with several other income streams but earns revenue though the podcast directly with sponsorships, fees to appear on his show and promotion and sales of affiliate products.

**HELPFUL WEBSITES**

1) Audacity (www.audacity.com)

Audacity is an audio editing and recording software that is often used by beginners to record and edit podcast episodes because it is free.

2) Podbean (www.podbean.com)

To start a podcast, you need a podcast host that will store and distribute your podcast's audio files. They provide a podcast RSS feed that you then submit to Apple and others. There are many services available but Podbean stands out because they offer unlimited bandwidth starting at $9/month and have an advertising marketplace that connects you with potential sponsors.

3) AudioJungle (www.audiojungle.com)

There are plenty of places to find free audio files online (we'll talk about them later in our YouTube strategy) but if you're going to be using a sound for a commercial purpose it's best to invest and purchase rights to a sound. I recommend searching AudioJungle since they have many affordable files as low as $5. They also have a monthly freebie you can grab that's a little higher quality than what you'd find on a free site.

4) Podcast Guests (www.podcastguests.com)

I love this website. They have a competitor that focuses on radio and interviews but they're just not even in the same ballpark. Podcast hosts and guests alike can use this platform to connect with each other. I've found no less than 20 interviews through this service and pay to have myself listed as a travel expert on their podcast guest directory.

5) The Podcast Host (www.thepodcasthost.com)

If you're just starting out and looking for a website that breaks down the who, what, where, when and how of podcasting, this blog is it.

**DOWNSIDE:**

You have to be smart to monetize. Most podcasts do not make money and if they do, it's far from a living wage. If you're expecting to get rich just with a podcast, you're going to be disappointed. It's an unbelievable platform to grow your audience since your episodes are found by new listeners years after they're published but you need to be prepared to direct those listeners into some sort of click funnel or email list so you can monetize them with additional products like courses or paid memberships.

**YOU KNOW YOU MADE IT WHEN:**

The average podcast gets less than 150 downloads in the first 30 days. You know you made it when you have 3,000+ downloads in the first 30 days, putting you in the top 10% of podcasters overall.

Your show is so popular that you attract high quality guests and grow exponentially every time, leveraging the power of their lists to promote your show. You have high-end brand partnerships that you're proud to work with and pay you well for a few seconds of airtime.

You're recognized by others in your field as an industry leader and frequently attend podcasting conferences and events because it feels like catching up with old friends.

**Strategy No. 8: Monthly Subscription/Membership**

This is the holy grail of an online business because instead of constantly having to find new customers you can just recharge existing customers. Not to mention, you know exactly how much money you'll have coming in every month based on your member count.

People are utilizing this strategy in several ways. Some are offering paid Facebook groups to network with influential individuals in a given field. There's one particular public relations group people gladly pay to get into because of the opportunities posted there. Others are offering a mail-based subscription, where they send a box of curated items to your house every month.

The idea is to gather a community around a service, product or topic and then charge for the value you provide that community on a dedicated platform.

**PAY RATE:**

What you make will depend on what you charge. Maybe you only charge $5/month because you run a group on how to get out debt and you know your audience is limited on funds. Maybe you charge $100/month for membership because you're offering a premium service.

When it comes to monthly charges, most subscription services won't exceed $100 unless you're offering one-on-one consulting or the opportunity to advance your member's financial status considerably.

For context, Birchbox costs $15/month for new subscribers. Let's say each box costs them $5 to make and ship provided people volunteer their samples to be included in the box for exposure. With only 1,000 subscribers, that's $10,000 every single month on repeat, coming out $120,000/year. You can see how easily something like this can scale. Currently, the company has 2.5 million subscribers.

**WHO IT'S SUITED FOR:**

You are consistent and dependable. People know they can count on you to deliver what you promise when you say you will, every month without fail. You're also a planner. You schedule out your tasks well in advance and are organized. You are energized by having to answer questions, not drained by it. You can be flexible and adapt your business model to technological changes and advancements.

**SUCCESS STORIES:**

My favorite example of a successful monthly subscription model is Scott's Cheap Flights. This is a multi-million dollar business with almost no start-up costs or advertising expenses. When Scott Keyes found a cheap flight to Milan one day, his friends asked him to let him know when he came across another good deal. He started sending emails to a small group of people and before he knew it that list grew to more than 2 million subscribers. He now employs a team of 30+ employees, all of whom work remotely.

Scott makes his money off a premium flight alert model. People sign up to be on the list for free but they only get a small percentage of the overall deals. Those who like what they see can go premium and pay $59/year to get all the deals. The list has grown thanks to referrals, word of mouth and media coverage. They don't pay for advertisements. It's such a smart business model that no less than 2 dozen other companies have popped up in the last 2 years trying to replicate his strategy.

On a smaller scale but equally ingenious is Carly Campbell from Mommy on Purpose. When Pinterest announced that it would be prioritizing "new images" on the platform, many content creators panicked. Carly saw this and set up a monthly subscription service where for $15 she sends out 30 new pin templates every month. If 500 people sign up for that service, she's making $7,500 a month for a task that ultimately takes no more than 3-5 hours of her time. This model has no startup costs, can be executed completely online and is so affordable that it's an easy and effective fix for her audience.

**HELPFUL WEBSITES**

1) Cratejoy (www.cratejoy.com)

If you're interested in starting a subscription box, you can do so through Cratejoy. It's an online platform that allows users to manage websites and subscriptions through their software, marketplace and support staff. They take a hefty cut of your profits but if you're just starting out and want to reach a bigger audience it's a good way to go.

2) ConvertKit (www.convertkit.com)

To do this business well you really need to focus on email more than most. You can use any system but ConvertKit is well set up for funnels and automations and only bills you based on subscribers and doesn't allow or charge for duplicates like their competitor Mailchimp.

3) MemberPress (www.memberpress.com)

This is a WordPress plugin that allows you to host a paid membership on your own website.It'll help you track subscriptions, sell digital downloads payments and take payments with ease. The program uses PayPal, Stripe and Authorize.net so all payments are processed and stored on a site separate from yours, important for security reasons.

4) Mighty Networks (www.mightynetworks.com)

If you're looking for a place to host your community outside of Facebook with more features and a dedicated support team, consider Mighty Networks. The platform is meant to gather your community in one place, providing everything from courses and webinars, a calendar of events, a forum where you can hold discussions, a feed of recent member posts and more. Prices range from free to $83 a month for the business plan.

5) Kajabi (www.kajabi.com)

This is an all-in-one membership site and platform that allows you to build you own website for your brand and have access to a private community area for members. It's one of the more expensive platforms with prices starting at $149/month but they don't take a fee from any of your subscriptions.

**DOWNSIDE:**

Scott Keyes is the exception to this rule but marketing is key to success here. So much so that you may start to feel consumed by it and resent the obligation to grow your community. There's also a limit to how much you can do on your own before you need to hire help. Finally, depending on what you offer (especially if it's a collection of curated physical products) your production and shipping costs could get high, leaving you with little net profit.

**YOU KNOW YOU MADE IT WHEN:**

You have a product or service that people just can't get enough of. They're willing to pay you for it regularly, with some people even wanting to pay extra to get increased access. You bill existing customers every month and have excellent retention rates. Your customer acquisition cost is next to nothing because you've been featured on major news outlets and used bloggers and affiliates to help get the word out.

You have a team that handles the day-to-day management and interaction with the community. You make special appearances as the founder but overall, it's a subscription set up under your name that allows you to sit back and collect recurrently.

## Strategy No. 9: YouTube Channel

YouTube is the #1 online video streaming service in the world, surpassing the numbers of users on Netflix, Hulu and Amazon Prime *combined*.

You know who the star of YouTube is? You! This platform has led to the discovery of famous recording artists like Justin Beiber, Shawn Mendes and Carly Rae Jepsen.

**PAY RATE:**

Once you hit 1,000 subscribers and 4,000 public watch hours in the last year, you can apply for the YouTube Partner Program to make money from ads hosted on your videos before it plays. Advertisers pay anywhere from $.10-$.30 per view but YouTube takes a cut (45%). On average, YouTuber creators make $4.18 per 1,000 views.

**WHO IT'S SUITED FOR:**

You like to be in front of the screen. You have a big personality and have always thought you should have a camera crew following you around.

You have a presence and way of connecting with others, whether it's making them laugh, inspiring them or teaching them something. You are dedicated to becoming a YouTube star and are able to keep a strict schedule. You don't mind paying a lot of money for something (in this case, electronics) so long as you you're getting the best quality.

**SUCCESS STORIES:**

My friends Jim and May at Spanish and Go have a YouTube channel with more than 90k subscribers. They make a full-time living off their ad revenue and related offerings like Spanish learning trips abroad. Jim was a professional videographer prior to making the transition which helped ease the learning curve.

**HELPFUL WEBSITES**

1) Adobe Photoshop (www.adobe.com)

Photoshop is part of the Adobe Creative Suite and is how you can cut (lasso) out pictures or still shots from your video to make custom video cover and thumbnail. It's important that you have an attractive cover to make your video stand out amongst search results and generate clicks.

2) Canva (www.canva.com)

If you don't want to invest in the Adobe Creative Suite, Canva is a great tool for YouTubers and content creators generally. They have free images and templates you can use to create promotional graphics like your YouTube cover, with branded images and colors. It's easy to use and generates a professional result.

3) Epidemic Sound (www.epidemicsound.com)

Epidemic sound is a collection of music that has already been paid for. You subscribe to their site to access the audio files for your own video. The alternative is to use YouTube Audio Library, which has free songs and sound effects but is somewhat limited in its selection. If your audio is not properly acquired or licensed, your video will be flagged and your account could face sanctions.

4) TubeBuddy (www.tubebuddy.com)

TubeBuddy is a paid keyword research program that lets you find out the exact terms people search for so you can tailor your title, video description and tags to fit those results. Keyword research makes all the difference. If YouTube doesn't know to show your video in response to a specific search term, it could be the most helpful video ever but unless it goes viral elsewhere no one will ever find it.

5) The Social Media Examiner (www.socialmediaexaminer.com)

There are many technical aspects to launching a YouTube channel that cannot be covered in depth in this book, such as using cards, broadcasting with YouTube Live, ways to increase your watch time, etc. This website has a ton of helpful posts and videos, just type in "YouTube" in the search box in the upper right hand corner to see everything in list form.

**DOWNSIDE:**

To do well on this platform you need to post consistently, like daily. This means that if you're a full-time YouTuber, you're spending a minimum of 8 hours a day producing and editing videos. There are exceptions, with some video formats taking less time to work on than others like just talking head or stream of conscious videos versus tutorials, guides or anything with special effects, B-roll or music.

**YOU KNOW YOU MADE IT WHEN:**

You're a well-known YouTube personality. You have a large following of tens (or hundreds) of thousands of people that eagerly await your new videos. You've had several posts go viral and are frequently invited as a VIP guest to functions thanks to your internet clout. You make good money from YouTube ads but even better money from brand sponsorships thanks to your audience.

You have tens (if not hundreds) of thousands of subscribers who eagerly await your new content and share and comment the moment it goes live. All of this translates to a blue check mark verifying you on IG, TikTok and Twitter. Congratulation! You're internet famous now.

## Strategy No. 10: E-Commerce

E-commerce is the buying and selling of goods online through a digital store, either hosted on a third party platform or on your own website. You can sell digital or physical products. If you're worried about packaging and shipping costs and time, you can adopt a dropshipping model wherein someone orders an item from your store, then you order the item from a third party wholesaler or manufacturer and have it delivered straight to your customer.

**PAY RATE:**

While we're all familiar with the big players in this space (Amazon, eBay, Zappos), the average e-commerce store can expect to bring in roughly $40k in its first year and revenue can go well into the seven figures by the third year.

**WHO IT'S SUITED FOR:**

You are a fan of testing. You like marketing and all it entails and get psyched about tweaking ads and copy to maximize your return on investment.

You have an entrepreneurial instinct and can identify trends early on. You're not afraid to make changes to your business model depending on the nature of the market and understand that you have to spend money to make money sometimes

**SUCCESS STORIES:**

When two friends, Casey Elsass and Morgen Newman, had the idea to create a chili-infused honey, they had no idea it would become the signature item of their new e-commerce store. In its first year, the store generated more than $170,000 from one product – their Bees Knees Spicy Honey. Since then they've changed their website name and are now Bushwick Kitchen. They've also expanded their product offerings to include maple syrup, totes and bags and gift sets.

## HELPFUL WEBSITES

1) Shopify (www.shopify.com)

Shopify is one of the biggest platforms for selling your products online. It's where brands like Kylie Cosmetics and Crabtree & Evelyn are hosted. You can completely customize your sales page and they collect orders and credit card payments on your behalf.

2) Oberlo (www.oberlo.com)

If you're using Shopify, consider going with Oberlo for any dropshipping needs. Oberlo is an app that allows you to import, sell and ship items from AliExpress directly to your customer. It's good for beginners because of the price. If you want more customized products sourced from Etsy stores and the like, consider Spocket instead.

3) WooCommerce (www.woocommerce.com)

WooCommerce is a WordPress plugin that allows you to set up an e-commerce platform on your own website. This could be a good option if you already have an established site with lots of traffic as visitors can just pop into your digital store while on your page. It is set up so that you accept payments directly, usually through PayPal.

4) Ecommerce CEO (www.ecommerceceo.com)

If you're just getting started, this website has helpful guides and free resources that will come in handy you're setting up your store. They cover everything from marketing tips to product research strategies.

5) Commerce Gurus (www.commercegurus.com)

In addition to quick-start guides and software reviews, this website has a theme that is specifically designed for the WooCommerce plugin called Shoptimizer. It has cool features like a call back option, trust badges and slide-up sales notifications.

**DOWNSIDE:**

Your revenue will be subject to market demands so you need to be able to predict what people will want to buy. There is a lot of competition out there so it can be hard to make your store stand out. Marketing is going to make up a large part of your start-up budget. To start an e-commerce business, it's recommended you have at least $1,000 initially to invest in marketing and design costs. Once you are launched, you'll also have to deal with frequent returns/refunds/exchanges since customers can't try your product before they buy it.

**YOU KNOW YOU MADE IT WHEN:**

You have a popular online store (or multiple stores) selling items at high margins with minimal investment or involvement on your behalf. You have shipping down to a science and are able to offer prompt delivery around the world at minimal costs. You enjoy your website and are passionate about the products you sell so it's easy to attract and engage others.

## Strategy No. 11: Private Coaching

Private coaching is alluring because it's cutting through the noise and getting right to the heart of the matter. People will pay for an expert to hold their hand through a process, life stage or new initiative, and they'll pay handsomely for it.

Most successful people turn to coaching at some point because of the potential to charge high rates. You can do one-on-one or group coaching depending on your preference, or both and offer group coaching as a more affordable introductory option. You can do coaching in any field so long as you have expertise and/or training, from physical training to mental health coaching and everything in between.

Popular areas of expertise for coaches include business, leadership, career, personal improvement, spirituality, family and romantic relationships, organization and more.

**PAY RATE:**

Beginner coaches can charge $50-$100 per hour. Intermediate coaches charge around $200/hour. Expert or celebrity coaches can charge by the thousands.

**WHO IT'S SUITED FOR:**

You like to lead by example and inspire others. You are a good listener and make people feel heard. You don't mind explaining things step-by-step, sometimes multiple times over, to help others replicate your success. You like to learn and stay on top of trends in your industry. You are high energy and are not afraid to put yourself out there.

**SUCCESS STORIES:**

One coach everyone knows is Marie Forleo. Marie runs B-School, a high end group coaching program that costs $2,000 for 8 weeks. She comes in to answer live Q&A's. To date she's graduated more than 40,000 entrepreneurs from the program.

Another example is Lana Shlafer, a manifestation and life coach. Lana holds small group, in-person and online MasterMind events where she helps people work through their struggles and offers her insight and guidance.

**HELPFUL WEBSITES**

1) International Coaching Federation (www.coachingfederation.org)

While you don't need to be certified to be a coach, it certainly helps you stand out in a saturated space. The International Coaching Federation ("ICF") offers different levels of certification, from associate to master, based on your training and experience. You need a minimum of 60 training hours to qualify. You can also become a member for $245/year to enjoy free resources, discounted credentialing applications, continuing coach education and be included in their online database of certified coaches.

2) HARO (www.helpareporter.com)

Short for Help a Reporter Out, HARO is a site where journalist go to find sources for their articles. As a coach, it helps to have publicity and media features that you can list on your website for added credibility. HARO sends out three emails a day, in the morning/afternoon/night, with journalist requests for sources. They're time sensitive so you have to answer quickly but this is the easiest way to make your way into major outlets like Forbes or USA Today.

3) Coach Training Alliance (www.coachtrainingalliance.com)

There are countless brands offering training programs to help you gain ICF certification. Typically, they take several months and cost an average of $3,000. One of the biggest companies is Coach Training Alliance. In addition to their paid program they have free resources such as a podcast, webinars and blog with instructional posts. They guarantee that you'll have clients by the end of 6 months and are ICF accredited.

4) GoToWebinar (www.gotomeeting.com)

One of the best ways to find new clients is to host free webinars where you give away value and hook attendees into signing up for your services. GoToWebinar is great because it allows you to set up on-demand webinars where people pick from a list of available times. Also, you can play a pre-recorded webinar so you only have to record the content once and can use it as a lead magnet over and over again.

5) LinkedIn (www.linkedin.com)

Another way to get clients is through LinkedIn. Make sure your title clearly states that you are a coach. Join a professional group and contribute to it regularly. Post one suggestion or tip daily to solve a struggle amongst your ideal clients. You can also reach out to 2nd or 3rd degree connections via private message, referencing your common friend.

**DOWNSIDE:**

Your business is dependent on getting clients so you constantly have to be networking and marketing yourself. You also have to deliver a transformation – people don't go to a coach to feel heard and understood, they go to a therapist for that. When you book a new client, it's because they think you can change their life for the better and you have to be up for that challenge. If you fail you provide a transformation you risk an unsatisfied customer, poor review and loss of trust and interest.

**YOU KNOW YOU MADE IT WHEN:**

You have a dedicated group of clients who respect your work and sing your praises to others. You can sell your services at different price ranges, offering pre-recorded courses for a few hundred dollars to arm up your leads and pitch them your big sell.

## Strategy No. 12: Travel Planner or Guide

Being a travel planner/guide is a dream job for many. Not only do you spend your days learning about fabulous places around the world, you often get to visit yourself and are paid to do so.

I want to encourage you to start an independent travel or tour company. While there are agencies like InteleTravel that will promise you the world, the gig of "travel agent" still requires you to hustle to find your own clients. Not to mention, those companies are MLM-based meaning there's incentives for members to recruit you and for you to recruit others. Agents are notoriously underpaid, averaging $36k/year on commission for sales grossing $800k or more.

The better strategy is to host small group tours or coordinate large international trips through your own platform. If you're worried about the logistics and concerned you won't be able to manage all the tourism contacts, start small and go local. Offers tours of your own town and coordinate with small businesses. Once you get a feel for how the process works it'll be easy to scale and hire additional guides.

**PAY RATE:**

Tour providers make their money in the margins. If you're hosting a walking tour for $30 and only spending $5 on a snack along the way, that's $25 profit for every person on your tour. If you're charging $3,000/pp for a 10-day trip that's costing $2,500/pp and bringing 5 people with you, that's $2,500. In either case, price your services accordingly so you can cover expenses, have a cushion for unexpected costs and still make a profit, all while providing value to your client. Piece of cake!

**WHO IT'S SUITED FOR:**

You are an adventurer. You love to go to new places and travel excites you. You also like people and don't mind dealing with big groups. You are patient and can solve problems quickly. You expect that guests attending the trip will have more than one issue come up and rely on you (or your staff) at all times of the day or night.

You love to research and read reviews thoroughly before making a purchase. You can explain to someone all of their options in a way that is simple and accurate. People trust your opinion and look to you for advice when they're making a big life decision or investment of money. You are generally friendly, likeable and able to communicate effectively with local partners despite language and cultural barriers.

**SUCCESS STORIES:**

Carol Knain is a former flight attendant and founder of World Traveler Wish List, a small group tour company that specializes in providing bucket list experiences around the world. Since Carol is an experiences traveler she skipped the middleman and started her own website, offering the ability to book and reserve trips online with a down payment. She then uses the down payments to help secure lodging, transportation and activities at the destination.

Carol goes on all the trips herself as the trip host/leader. She is constantly traveling, organizing one or two dozen trips a year to locations like Egypt, the Galapagos Islands and the Maldives. She gets to travel for free and makes a minimum of $1,000 net profit over the course of a 7-10 day trip.

On a smaller scale, Brian Cicioni from I May Roam offers food tours around cities like New York and Philadelphia through Eventbrite and promotes them on his travel blog. Also, Amanda Mouttaki is an expat living in Morocco who started Marrakech Food Tours. While Brian leads his tours, Amanda hires local guides. There are many ways to do this depending on the level of guest interaction you desire.

## HELPFUL WEBSITES

1) Get Your Guide (www.getyourguide.com)

If you want to host a local tour or activity, consider listing it on Get Your Guide. It could be something as simple as leading a walking tour of your favorite city murals. The benefit of Get Your Guide is that they're available in over 100 countries and have a more international audience. They take 20-30% of your profits so make sure to price accordingly.

2) Viator (www.viator.com)

Viator is similar to Get Your Guide but targets a more U.S. audience. They take 20% of your profits and also offer a program for travel agents where you get 8% commission on any trips you sell (if you're still intent on trying the agent route).

3) Google AdWords (www.ads.google.com)

While I recommend you work on long-term strategies that bring you warm leads for free (i.e. opt-ins, a blog, podcast, etc.) those just starting out will find value in Google AdWords. You can set up a campaign to target certain search terms so that your website comes out at the top of results. You set a budget and pay on a cost per click basis.

4) Purposeful Nomad (www.purposefulnomad.com)

I recommend you start small when you're hosting your first trip to test your business model and concept. If you're nervous about doing everything yourself and want to work with a company that has established itineraries and contacts, consider Purposeful Nomad. A lot of group tour providers cut corners but Purposeful Nomad aims to provide a quality experience and will host your trip for you, you just market it and bring the people along.

**DOWNSIDE:**

The danger with this strategy lies in turning something you love and escape to into a job. Travel will not be as fun when you're responsible for the diversion of 12 other people.

**YOU KNOW YOU MADE IT WHEN:**

Not only do you get to help others find and fund their dream trips, you get to go along for the ride with them! You spend your days planning the perfect sunrise photo shoot at the Taj Mahal, finding the best flower bath in Bali and trekking glaciers in Argentina. Best of all? These trips are all expenses paid and you actually make a profit.

Over time, you grow a dedicated and knowledgeable staff that allows you to scale your services and offer more tours, without you needing to be on them. Now you just sit back, travel as you see fit and watch the money roll in.

## Strategy No. 13: Online Courses

Do you know something most other people don't? If so, there's someone online willing to pay you to teach it to them. The worldwide e-learning market is estimated to be worth $325 billion by 2025. Don't miss your chance to get a piece of that pie!

**PAY RATE:**

Generally, courses will cost anywhere from $50-$200. There are also high-end courses (four figures and up) but those tend to include one-on-one work and fall into the category of coaching. Bear in mind that people are most likely to invest big money in a course when they believe they will benefit financially from it.

**WHO IT'S SUITED FOR:**

You are able to break down complicated concepts into small, digestible bits of information.

**SUCCESS STORIES:**

Melyssa Griffin turned her Pinterest knowledge into a 6-fiure course on Teachable. Her course did well for because she provided insight into a social media platform touted as the "secret weapon" for getting traffic to your site, with exponentially higher click through rates than competitors like Instagram or Facebook. She was able to sell the dream of making money through increased Pinterest traffic.

Rick Shetty from Daddy Blogger is on a mission to be the first family to visit every country in the world. He has more than a dozen courses on Udemy on everything from branding to fatherhood.

## HELPFUL WEBSITES

1) Teachable (www.teachable.com)

Teachable is one of the best platforms for hosting your course. They have the option to customize your sales page and give you direct access to the email addresses of people who purchase your course. They have a support team on call and are constantly hosting online webinars and live training events. You set your own prices on Teachable and are responsible for your own marketing. Paid plans start at $39/month. The more you pay monthly, the less you pay in transaction fees for each sale.

2) Udemy (www.udemy.com)

Udemy has more than 50 million students and is your best option for reaching a large audience if you're not willing to invest in marketing or don't have an established fan base yet. Your content will be found by people searching the site (in contrast to Teachable where people have to know the link to your page to find it). They deeply discount classes periodically and you have no control over that. Still, 10% of something is better than 100% of nothing.

3) Skillshare (www.skillshare.com)

Skillshare is a membership-based service that has a lot of creative classes in topics like photography and design. Students pay $10/month for unlimited classes so you have no control over the pricing. You must have a minimum of 30 minutes watched in all your classes each month to be eligible for payment. From there, you're compensated based on an algorithm that takes into account how many students enrolled, projects created by your students and the total number of people who signed up for Skillshare in general that month. Compensation can range from $200-$3,000 a month. If you promote your course and get a lot of new signups and reviews you will be marked as "trending" and have increased visibility on the platform.

4) Thinkific (www.thinkific.com)

Of all the platforms, Thinkific most resembles an online classroom and is scalable for multiple instructors, admin and support staff. There are unique features like goal setting, tracking and customized learning environments. Paid plans start at $49/month.

5) Podia (www.podia.com)

Podia allows you to host not just courses but membership sites and webinars as well. You can also sell PDF downloads or Excel tracking sheets. Podia has no fees and gives you access to your users so you can contact them directly. You can sell on your own storefront and get a custom domain name.

**DOWNSIDE:**

It can be hard to stand out amongst all the courses being offered online. Also, even if you create a high-value course it's possible a third party like Udemy will ultimately knock your course down to $10. If you're not hosted on a large site like Udemy that has its own user database, you'll need to work hard at driving eyes to your course on other platforms.

**YOU KNOW YOU MADE IT WHEN:**

You launch a course and in a weekend, you make more than you did in a year at your old 9-5 job. You sold a course to 200 people at $200 each and made $40,000. You can do the same launch year after year and target your existing clients with a new product. If they liked your course on French desserts, they'll love your course on mastering the art of flambé. Over time, you build a collection of digital courses that bring you steady passive income years after you complete them.

# CHAPTER THREE

# *Blog and Social Media*

> *"Entrepreneurs jump off a cliff and build parachutes on the way down."*
> *— Reid Hoffman*

### Strategy No. 14: Affiliate Marketing

Affiliate marketing is when you promote someone else's product and make a commission from the sale. You can place affiliate links anywhere, from a YouTube video description to your IG profile bio. It helps if you're linking to relevant products somewhere that your audience is looking for a solution.

If you have a blog post on the best credit card to open, for example, you should include as many affiliate links as you can so that if people decide to open any of those cards after reading your post, you'll be credited (and more importantly – paid!).

You don't need to be a blogger or social media influencer to promote affiliate links, you just need access to an interested audience. For instance, if you're an accountant you could recommend a particular software or bookkeeping program and earn money every time one of your customers signs up. Just be aware that when you use affiliate links you must disclose the connection and might need to get permission from higher-ups depending on your job's policies.

**PAY RATE:**

Most affiliate programs pay anywhere from 5-10% of the sale you make for them. You need to be aware of cookie tracking, a.k.a. how long after the initial click the company will attribute the sale to you. If the customer has to make a purchase immediately when they click for the sale to count, you're not going to make as much from that program and will want to seek a partnership with better terms.

**WHO IT'S SUITED FOR:**

You are a salesperson. You are persuasive and trustworthy. You have an audience that looks to you for recommendations on the best products to buy. Your presence is established somewhere you could easily market to your audience, like an email list or blog. You are a fan of data and tracking numbers. You live for analytics reports. You can make promotion seem natural and seamless, not forced or awkward.

**SUCCESS STORIES:**

One successful person in this field is Sharon Gurley from Digital Nomad Wannabe. Sharon runs a course on affiliate marketing and has detailed posts and guides on her website to help you get started.

## HELPFUL WEBSITES

1) CJ Affiliate (www.cj.com)

This is one of the biggest affiliate networks out there. They work with more than 300 merchants, such as Home Depot and Apple. The way it works is you create a program and then apply to individual affiliate networks. If you already have a relationship with an affiliate manager, they can also send you an invitation to join their program. You accept the terms, integrate the links on your platforms and start earning.

2) Impact (www.impact.com)

Formed in 2008 by the former founders of CJ Affiliate, Impact is a solution-based digital marketing agency that wants to put creators in touch with brands that make sense for them. They have a high-quality, vetted marketplace and stricter application process.

3) ShareASale (www.shareasale.com)

This is a large affiliate marketing network that's been in business for almost 20 years. They were acquired by Awin and have reputable brands worldwide. Pay rates and commission will vary depending on the merchant.

4) Ultimate Bundles (www.ultimatebundles.com)

This is one of the highest paying affiliate programs out there, offering a 40% commission on each sale. You can either contribute to a bundle or agree to promote a bundle. A bundle is a collection of products, downloads and webinars on a certain topic. They're offered at such a discounted rate that you're able to give value to your audience while bringing in a good chunk of revenue.

5) ClickFunnels (www.clickfunnels.com)

ClickFunnels is a program that helps you put together sales funnels from scratch. You don't need to have a separate website, email provider or online shop – it has everything for you on one platform so you can sell products, host webinars and create membership sites. Prices start at $97/month.

**DOWNSIDE:**

To be honest, I would suggest you create your own products rather than rely on affiliate marketing for your full-time income because you're going to be selling hard and not reaping the bulk of the profits. However, if you already have a product that you're selling and can include affiliate links therein, then it's a nice bonus.

For instance, let's say you have a course on how to increase your credit score by 100 points in one year. If within that course you include your comparison of the best credit cards with affiliate links, then the commission can be seen as the cherry on top of your digital entrepreneur sundae.

Otherwise, it takes time to build enough traffic where you'll see significant gains from affiliate income. It's also possible that you'll not be credited for a sale depending on the cookie and tracking policies of a particular brand. You're also not given any data about the customer who ultimately made a purchase so you're unable to retarget them in the future.

**YOU KNOW YOU MADE IT WHEN:**

You've sprinkled high-earning affiliate links throughout all of your online content. You are partnered with relevant brands that provide value to your audience so recommending them feels natural. Sales are always happening in the background without you constantly having to promote. You don't have to create your own products and so you have very little time or money invested into this income stream.

## Strategy No. 15: Advertising Revenue

Advertising can be found wherever there is an audience. That's why you have to watch 4 seconds of an obligatory commercial on YouTube before it plays a video or why radio shows have "short breaks" to help them pay the bills.

Advertisers pay for the privilege of getting in front of a targeted group of people. While you can monetize from anywhere, one of the easiest ways is through a blog or website since there are established programs you can apply for once you reach a set traffic threshold.

**PAY RATE:**

Blog advertising programs are paid on an RPM basis where you make a set amount per thousand people that come to your site. If you have an RPM of $30, for instance, and you had 3,000 people visit your site that day, your earnings would be $90. There are bloggers making 6-figures off advertising revenue alone.

**WHO IT'S SUITED FOR:**

You are willing and able to follow a formula to drive traffic to your site. You don't need catchy titles or puns – you're OK writing for Google. You can't get enough of search engine optimization and get a thrill every time you see numbers rising on a chart.

**SUCCESS STORIES:**

I'm going to list myself here (no shame!). In February 2018 I finally reached the numbers I needed to apply for an advertising network. I went from 10,000 page views a month to more than 100,000 page views a month, all in less than a year. During that time, I was making an average of $2,000 a month in ad revenue. To be clear, I could have slept all day and still made $80-$100.

The best part? This success can be easily scaled or replicated on more than one website.

**HELPFUL WEBSITES**

1) Mediavine (www.mediavine.com)

Mediavine is a publisher network that you can apply for once you have a website that passes 50,000 sessions/month. They run all of your ads from their platform – you simply decide where you want the ads to show up on your site and they source the brands and content. They are very publisher friendly and have a team that's dedicated to helping blogs succeed.

2) Ezoic (www.ezoic.com)

If your traffic doesn't quite reach the 25k sessions mark yet, consider signing up with Ezoic for ad placement and management. They require a minimum of 10k visits a month. Note that they RPMs will be lower than Mediavine's.

3) Keysearch (www.keysearch.co)

If you're creating content online and aren't researching first to see the demand for certain keywords, you're doing yourself a disfavor. Maybe you wrote on article on the best chili recipes, but there's 10 times more traffic for the term "vegetarian chili recipes" or "chili recipes instant pot." By doing keyword research on a site like Keyword first, you can know the demand for content before you begin creating it, ensuring more eyes on your posts.

4) Make Traffic Happen (www.maketraffichappen.com)

This is a community that helps you learn about and master SEO so that your blog posts will show up on page 1 of Google search results. They have bloggers of all niches in a robust Facebook group and two SEO books I highly recommend. They also offer in-person courses and training for anyone needing a extra technical assistance. Using their blog post optimization tactics, I went from 10,000 to 100,000 page views in 10 months.

5) Moz (www.moz.com)

Moz is a site that allows you to check backlinks and domain authority for your site, two indicators as to the likelihood that your site will show up at the top of search results. You need to create an account to use the site and get 10 free domain explorer searches per month.

**DOWNSIDE:**

The downside of relying on advertising revenue is that you're subject to income fluctuations as the search volumes for a particular term change. For instance, if you have a site that focuses on winter sports and recreation, you're likely to experience a dip in traffic and income during the summer months.

**YOU KNOW YOU MADE IT WHEN:**

You make money in your sleep. You wake up every day to increased traffic and RPM's, meaning higher payouts. Blog posts that you've written and updated throughout the years rank on the first page of Google and bring you steady traffic without you having to invest in advertising or be constantly promoting on social media.

### Strategy No. 16: Summits

A summit is a gathering of people for a common reason, typically to learn or discuss something. Hosting an online summit is one of the quickest ways to generate revenue. In contrast to a course, you don't have to spend months recording video or producing content. Your summit consists of you handing over the virtual stage to a guest who presents an hour-long session about their expertise.

You can choose to host the summits yourself through your own website and channels or you can go through a third party summit hosting website with built-in features to promote, execute and follow up on leads after the event.

Live summits and retreats are a natural step up once you've perfected the online model. People will be eager for a chance to connect with you in person. Often, these "Mastermind" groups are productive and fun, with attendees returning year after year and forming a community.

You could also form your own in-person conference after a few successful summits and charge for access to the recordings after. Alessandra Torre does this with Inkers Con, a writer's conference. Another example is the Travel Con conference launched by Nomadic Matt.

**PAY RATE:**

For an online summit, it's typical to offer access to the live sessions for free (and up to one week after they air) and then have people pay for continuing access to all the sessions after that time. Typically, it's about $100-$200 for access, per person. If you have a summit with 20 guests, all of whom have email lists of over 10,000 people, that's a reach of 200,000 people. Even with a conservative 3% conversion rate, you can make $6,000-$12,000 off a one-time event. You can compensate your attendees either with affiliate links, a one-time payment or promotion and exposure depending on the size of your audience.

For an in-person Mastermind retreat, the price typically falls between $3,000-$5,000 for a few days. For a conference, ticket prices fall between $200-$1,000 per person. These last two events will require overhead costs as you'll be paying for a meeting space, food, etc. For those reasons, an online summit is the best option if you're getting started don't have a lot of capital to pay up front.

## WHO IT'S SUITED FOR:

You are a social butterfly. You connect with and gather people easily. You like to be the host and don't mind planning elaborate parties. You have friends with many different skill sets. If you all went on a group trip, you would be the one making reservations and taking down payments.

## SUCCESS STORIES:

Bestselling author Christine Kloser hosts the wildly popular Transformational Author Summit. She gathers 10-30 experts with different specialties. The summit is up for a few days and then attendees pay for access to the recordings beyond the initial viewing period. This is a great way to build her list, make new contacts and generate significant income.

Christine doesn't have to write a book herself or create a 30-hour course – she just interviews the guests and posts their videos to the summit webpage. The guests even do most of the promotion and sales for her!

## HELPFUL WEBSITES

1) Hey Summit (www.heysummit.com)

If you need a place to host your summit, this is it. They help you create, manage, run and analyze your event from start to finish and have tools designed to deliver the best experience, including an email reminder and RSVP system for individual sessions.

2) vFairs (www.vfairs.com)

vFairs is a virtual events platform that allows you to host job shows, online trade shows, conferences and more. They have features like live streaming and an audience chat forum. You can also use the platform to hold an alumni or networking event.

3) Virtual Summit School (www.virtualsummitschool.com)

Virtual Summit School is taught by Bailey Richert, the self-proclaimed queen of summits. Her testimonials boast 5 and 6-figure returns. You can sign up for a free masterclass before committing to the program, a hefty investment at $997 but one of the few trainings of this type on the market.

4) Summit in a Box (www.summitinabox.co)

Run by Krista Miller, this website is a one-stop shop for all things related to virtual summits. There's a blog, free downloads, templates, one-on-one coaching and mentoring as well as a podcast called Summit Host Hangouts.

5) Vimeo (www.vimeo.com)

If you're looking to host videos on your own platform, you can use Vimeo. You have more control and a more professional look than you do with YouTube. For instance, you can remove the Vimeo logo from videos before you embed them somewhere.

**DOWNSIDE:**

To pull off a digital summit, you need to make sure the technology works without a hitch. You need strong WiFi and a program that will make things like timed releases and password protected content easy to manage. You need to vet your participants carefully to make sure they have a big enough audience and you might need to keep reminded them to share/promote with their audiences. It will also take time for you to set up and record the various presentations. If you don't execute it properly it can be a lot of time, effort and favors called in with not enough return on investment.

**YOU KNOW YOU MADE IT WHEN:**

You are a summit master! You can hold a major event quarterly online and get thousands of attendees, with a high conversion rate. You've made influential friends and are regarded as a leader in your industry because fans of your summit speakers see you front and center as the host. You appropriate their know, like and trust to you by extension and grow your email list and customers exponentially with each event.

### Strategy No. 17: Sponsored Content

Sponsored content is basically a marketing campaign. A brand pays you to test or review their product and in return, you promote it to your audience.

There are sponsorships available in every niche, from home décor to fitness. You are able to cold pitch brands by emailing their marketing department with your media kit and proposal, or you can join "influencer networks" that keep you apprised of paid campaigns.

You can make good money doing this, with some people being professional Instagrammers from brand sponsorships alone. If you're going to stand out amongst the growing talent pool, be professional in all of your endeavors. Have a polished media kit and know your statistics (age, location, gender, income and interests of your audience). Provide follow-up reports and case studies after a campaign is over so that the brand has numbers they can use for their reports.

One of the best ways to find sponsorships is to network with brand reps at live events and conferences. At the end of this book I include a list of top conferences to attend as a digital entrepreneur.

**PAY RATE:**

Sponsored posts can be very lucrative with pay rate varying on factors such as audience size, engagement and topic. Typically, when you're just starting out many companies will offer you a free product in exchange for your review.

As you grow, you can start to ask for compensation in addition to compensated products and experiences. There's no magic number at which you can start asking for monetary compensation. I recommend you always ask and negotiate for alternative perks, like an affiliate link or social media promotion on the brand's channels if there's no budget available.

Once you have tens, or hundreds, of thousands of followers you can charge anywhere from $500-$5,000 for a single post on Instagram. Currently, Instagram is the most lucrative social media platform.

As a blogger, I charge $500 per sponsored post on my website. Other platforms like Facebook and Twitter bring in about $200 per sponsored post.

**WHO IT'S SUITED FOR:**

People always ask you where you got your outfit from or what organizing products you use. When your loved ones are making a big purchase, they want to hear your opinion first. You are a go-getter. You don't mind constantly applying for partnerships, meeting new people at trade conferences and putting yourself out there.

**SUCCESS STORIES:**

Jessie Festa runs two successful websites – Epicurean Culture and her namesake blog, Jessie on a Journey. She's taken paid trips to destinations like Nepal and The Galapagos and collaborated with countless brands. She helps bloggers land sponsored posts and better monetize their channels through a private membership community called Travel Blog Prosperity. I'm a member and affiliate because I find her content practical and she's generous with her time and success secrets. Use the code "workfromhome" to try one month free.

**HELPFUL WEBSITES**

1) Influenster (www.influenster.com)

Influenster is the best place to go if you are just starting out and don't have many followers. They put together boxes of new products that companies are testing and want feedback on. You fill out a form for each campaign expressing your interest. If you're chosen, you get the box of products for free and are required to post pictures on your social media channels and leave reviews online. They work with major brands, from Nestle to Loreal.

2) TapInfluence (www.tapinfluence.com)

TapInfluence is an influencer marketing network. Content creators sign up and create a profile. They're then added to the marketplace. Marketers can search for people who match their project and extend a direct offer to work with them at a set price point or hold an open bidding process, taking offers from creators.

3) Fohr (www.fohr.com)

Fohr is an influencer network that has a bulletin you can click on to see a list of all currently active campaigns and sponsorships. If you feel you are a fit, you can click and apply to each one individually. Compensation ranges from a free product to $200 payment and is limited to posting on social media. It's rare that you'll see sponsorships paying more.

4) Perlu (www.perlu.com)

I like Perlu because it allows you to network not just with brands but other content creators as well. You can find diverse opportunities for collaboration here. You can also express your interest in working with one particular brand and be the first to get notified of any new campaigns.

5) Trend (www.trend.io)

Unlike the other platforms listed, Trend is invitation-only. You apply to join with your Instagram handle and examples of past partnerships. All collaborations are paid and they cater to micro-influencers with 5,000-50,000 followers.

**DOWNSIDE:**

It can be difficult to strike a balance between earning a profit and being true to your readers. When sponsors pay for you to work with them, they treat the content like a commercial and can take issue with negative feedback. This income is also unsteady. You may land a big contract in one month but not find another partnership for several more. Also, if you do enough of these you could start to annoy your audience by constantly promoting versus providing value.

**YOU KNOW YOU MADE IT WHEN:**

You make four (or five!) figures just for posting pictures with a product that you got for free. The real kicker is, you love the product so much you would have bought it anyway. If you're in the travel or food space, you visit the world's most luxurious vacation spots and restaurants and eat for free. You get to meet the chef and hotel manager and are treated like a VIP guest while still getting paid for your time.

If you're in the fashion and beauty industry, you get free clothes and makeup. You're invited to fashion shows and get early access to new products. If you get big enough and gain millions of followers, you might even be asked to launch your own makeup or clothing line.

# CHAPTER FOUR

# *Tech Skills Required*

*"Be nice to nerds. Chances are you'll end up working for one." - Bill Gates*

**Strategy No. 18: Buy and Sell Websites**

You remember in the introduction when we talked about emails being like houses online? Buying and selling domain names is the new real estate investment strategy. You can make good money flipping websites. You just have to know what "good bones" look like and how to estimate a site or domain name's value.

To differentiate between the two, a domain name is the web address, i.e. cool website dot com. The website itself is all of the content available once you reach the address. When buying and selling, the latter is worth more because it generates ongoing revenue.

**PAY RATE:**

You can buy a new domain name for $10 to $15 and then hold it until someone wants to pay a premium for that domain. For instance, there are people who bought up every variation of "Puerto Rico tours" available online and are just sitting on the names. When someone wants to open up a tour company, they'll have to reach out and negotiate a price with the domain name owner.

For a premium domain, that could be $1,000 and up. So, even if the purchaser spent $200 buying 20 domains, the sale of just one of those domain names would offset the costs and turn a sizeable profit.

When buying and selling websites, the general rule of thumb is that a website is worth what it makes in revenue over two years. That means that a site making $2,000 a month from advertising and affiliates would be worth around $48,000 on the market.

If you're someone with a knack for building web traffic and monetizing a site, you can create websites on several different topics with the goal of selling them once they reach a certain income threshold.

**WHO IT'S SUITED FOR:**

If you're getting into the domain name business, you're someone with an eye for trends. You are a good negotiator and don't mind sitting on investments until the time comes to cash them in.

**SUCCESS STORIES:**

Marc Andre is a finance blogger and founder of Blogging Wizard. He sold his first site, which earned six figures a year and consisted of quality articles contributed by financial consultants, for a half a million dollars. He's since replicated the process several times over, selling sites for $200k+.

## HELPFUL WEBSITES

1) Blogs for Sale (www.blogsforsale.co)

This is one of the few places online dedicated to selling only blogs. If you're a successful blogger with a track record of earning income on your site, you can list your website here. Alternatively, if you're looking to start a website and don't want to start from scratch, you could browse the available options and take over an existing site.

2) Flippa (www.flippa.com)

If you're looking to sell your site, you can list it on Flippa and entertain offers. I wouldn't necessarily recommend this marketplace for purchasing sites. There are a lot of scam and duplicate sites so if you do end up purchasing here make sure to do a thorough backlink audit, review the traffic and income and ask questions to the seller directly.

3) Empire Flippers (www.empireflippers.com)

Empire Flippers are the largest website brokers online, having sold more than $93 million worth of online businesses. Websites sell quickly here, in a matter of days or weeks, and they boast an 88% sales success rate. There is a vetting process and fee but if approved your listing gets shared on an email blast to 50k+ potential buyers. The process can take 2-4 weeks.

4) FE International (www.feinternational.com)

FE International is also brokerage firm. You express your interest in working with a broker and they send you questions to assess your site and its estimated worth on the marketplace. They ask you to prepare your own Profit & Loss Sheet and their valuation team gets back to you within a few days with a decision.

5) Exchange Marketplace (www.exchangemarketplace.com)

If you're looking to transact in e-commerce stores specifically, Exchange Marketplace is the place to be. Here, you can find, buy and sell online businesses built on Shopify specifically.

**DOWNSIDE:**

If you're selling your site, you need to be prepared to show an established revenue stream. Even when you get a generous offer, it can be hard to part with someone you've created and grown from scratch.

If you're buying a site, you need to be careful and do all our research before purchasing. If a site is being sold for $1200, you should expect revenues of $50/month or less.

**YOU KNOW YOU MADE IT WHEN:**

You are savvy about the website flipping process. You can spot a diamond in the rough when it's time to invest and know when to sell a site that's turning a profit. You make 5 or 6 figures for each transaction and have minimal day-to-day tasks of running your sites because you've hired help or chosen sites that don't require shipping and customer support.

## Strategy No. 19: Install and Customize WordPress Themes

WordPress is the pre-eminent platform for hosting a website. Most serious business owners will have a site but will have difficulty with installing and customizing a theme.

**PAY RATE:**

For designing a single page like a home page, web designers can charge anywhere from $200-$500. For designing a full website, you're looking at a minimum of $1,000.

**WHO IT'S SUITED FOR:**

You're someone with at least a rudimentary knowledge of coding. You have experience with mobile site speed, backlinks, email systems integration, etc. You don't need to know *all* the software and widgets out there but you need to be well acquainted with the ones you're utilizing.

**SUCCESS STORIES:**

Laura from Pixel Me Designs is a self-taught web designer and front end developer. She's worked with more than 500 clients and uses a custom Genesis theme. She also offers upsells like social media covers, logo design and branding consultations.

**HELPFUL WEBSITES**

1) Theme Forest (www.themeforest.net)

This site has hundreds of website themes and templates for you to choose from. Most themes come with the option of purchasing some type of support package and I highly recommend you invest in it, especially if you're buying one that's highly customizable and has a lot of features.

2) PipDig (www.pipdig.co)

If you need a blog theme that's easy to set up and has a beautiful aesthetic, browse the collection on PipDig. Most are priced between $50-$75, are customizable without need for coding and look professional -- great for blogs that are smaller or just starting out.

3) WordPress (www.wordpress.com)

WordPress is the premier platform for a blog or site. While there are competitors like Square Space, Wix and Blogger, if you intend to monetize with ads at some point it's recommended you work on WordPress. It's the industry standard so basing your skills in WordPress will make your services applicable to more people.

4) Elementor (www.elementor.com)

Elementor is a website builder that allows WordPress users to create and edit websites by using a drag and drop technique. It has a built-in responsive mode and makes it easy to put together a professional looking website with no prior experience. It's one of the most popular website builder tools on the market.

5) Code.org (www.code.org)

If you want to learn to code but find it mind-numbingly boring, Code.org is for you. This nonprofit association aims to teach computer science to students and has coding lessons where you can practice your skills by completing tasks like coding a dance video. Best of all, it's free to use.

**DOWNSIDE:**

You need to be aware of what you're doing, otherwise you could lose data on a site or open it up to malware. You will also need to be OK making revisions and taking direction from the site owner who may not always share your vision or understand your reasoning. You'll deal with competitors who might copy your ideas or undercut your price. If you take a project on at a flat rate and multiple revisions are required, your hourly rate could end up being far below what you'd normally charge.

**YOU KNOW YOU MADE IT WHEN:**

You are a sought-after web designer with more projects than you have time to take. You make stunning websites that portray the essence of a client's business and attract new leads on autopilot. You have developed a sense for design, organization and flow so the websites you create work seamlessly on desktop, tablet or mobile. You can charge 4 or 5 figures per site and own a business that fulfills your need to live creatively while ensuring financial freedom.

## Strategy No. 20: Graphic Design

There is a big demand for graphic design work online. Anyone attempting the income streams described in this book is going to need graphics for promotion, their social media channels, products, etc. What's more, it's hard to find quality graphics at a fair price.

This means that if you have design skills, are prompt on your delivery and can produce original artwork, there is an audience willing to pay you for your work.

**PAY RATE:**

The average salary for a graphic designer is $50,000/year. You can choose to work for a company as an employee or start your own freelance design business. If you opt to go the freelancing route, your pay will depend on the nature and extent of the projects you're working on, as well as the commission taken by any third party platforms. To give you context, the average payout for winning book cover design on 99Designs is about $200. Rates charged on a designer's personal website for the same task can be upwards of $1,000.

**WHO IT'S SUITED FOR:**

You are an artist at heart. You want to create, not worry about the business side of things. You can design stunning visuals in a short amount of time and have can get a good sense of what your clients want even if they're not great at providing detailed descriptions.

**SUCCESS STORIES:**

Michelle Fontaine is an award-winning graphic designer with more than 20 years of experience. She started her own freelance business online and offers her work through different artist websites. She has competitive rates, a quick turnaround time and customers across all fields and niches. She's established an impressive portfolio and list of testimonials, both of which help establish her credibility and attract new clients.

## HELPFUL WEBSITES

1) Awesome Web (www.ifyoucould.com)

If you're an experienced freelancer looking to skip the bidding war and land high-end clients, consider Awesome Web. They personally vet all their designers and have only 800 in their listings, compared to 99Design's 900k+. They don't take percentage fees from your project and run on a monthly subscription model instead.

2) Authentic Jobs (www.authenticjobs.com)

This is a job board made specifically for designers, developers and creative professionals.They have both full-time jobs and freelance positions available. You can search the listings and apply directly through the site by including your name, email, message and link to your portfolio.

3) Art Wanted (www.artwanted.com)

Art Wanted is a community where you can showcase your work and also list it for sale. It's meant to serve as inspiration and is a place to connect and communicate with other artists through group forums and discussion boards.

4) Hit Record (www.hitrecord.com)

Hit Record is an artist collective that was founded by Joseph Gordon-Levitt. The concept is to allow people to contribute to parts of a project and allow everyone to get paid. If you're a creative, I recommend you sign up and start by participating in one of the creative prompts.

5) Creative Planet Network (www.creativeplanetnetwork.com)

The Creative Planet Network is a website that has art news, tips, features and reviews. It's a handy resource for creatives and also has a job board/forum where you can find vacancies in graphic design.

**DOWNSIDE:**

It can be difficult to stand out as a designer and when freelancing, you're often competing and bidding against others who might steal your work. There's also a possibility the client you pitch your design to will turn down your offer, copy your idea and have someone make it for cheaper instead. It's a cutthroat industry so you need to be sure you take project deposits and have a contract outlining details like how many revisions you'll make and rights to any proposed designs.

**YOU KNOW YOU MADE IT WHEN:**

You make beautiful design concepts that are attention-grabbing and well executed. You love what you do and enjoy the creative process behind coming up with a new idea. You work well with clients and can translate their ideas into a finished product that exceeds their expectations. As a result, you come highly recommend and regularly land high-paying and ongoing projects.

## Strategy No. 21: Create an App

Have you ever played Angry Birds and thought, "how is possible this game makes so much money?" Creating a profitable app is easier than it looks.

While it helps to have coding skills or a talented developer on your team, it's not necessary. There are plenty of services that will help you create the app. The more important hurdle is coming up with a novel concept or improving on an existing idea.

If you already have a community or paid membership, an app could be an easy next step. You can have access to the same content in a quicker and more mobile-friendly format. Apps have also been shown to increase audience engagement.

As an example, travel bloggers could put together an app with city guides for a specific region. An e-commerce store could put together an app with coupons, daily specials the ability to pre-order items. A fashion consultant could make an app that mixes and matches pieces in your wardrobe. You get the drift.

Some general tips to keep in mind -- always add value. Create an app that is clean, attractive and easy to use. Don't overload the app with too much content all at once since that eats up battery life. Make sure it's user-friendly and easy for anyone to navigate regardless of age or tech background. Make it clear from the icon and name what your app is about. Offer free content but connect it back to any products or upsells you have available to maximize income.

Popular categories include games, mobile versions of magazines and newspapers, shopping, fitness and wellness, personalization tools (i.e. free wallpapers) and social media apps.

**PAY RATE:**

You can monetize an app directly by making it a paid download (one-time or recurring yearly/monthly subscription), offering paid extras inside the app, accepting sponsorships or hosting advertisements on the app. The top 25% of iOS app developers make $5,000/month. Only 16% of Android app developers reach that same threshold.

It's important to note that most of the top performing apps are owned by major corporations and that some companies have even been formed with the sole purpose of creating apps. Less than 1% of consumer mobile apps are financially successful. That said, if you're looking to make a full-time living off developing alone, the key is to have multiple apps.

Like podcasting, an app is much more commonly used by entrepreneurs and small business owners as a way to gain new followers and clients, reach a broader audience, connect with your community and link back to your related content.

**WHO IT'S SUITED FOR:**

You are a nerd and proud of it. You love to innovate, create and experiment. You don't mind testing and refining a product until it's the very best it can be. You have a vision for your app and money to invest in design, development and marketing. You trust people to work with you and have no problem delegating key aspects of your business. Also, you're big on researching, numbers and testing hypothesis – can't get enough of it.

**SUCCESS STORIES:**

The Albert App was founded in part by Daniel Bruce in an attempt to take the hassle out of invoicing, tracking expenses and bookkeeping for freelancers. It has since grown to be one of the top apps in the Apple store, ranking in the top 50 overall for finance. The app is free to download. The main source of revenue is Albert Genius, a subscription service aimed to save you money and increase your financial acuity.

The Name App was founded by Christian Perez to help users find domain names. The app compiles data already available online and partners with web hosts to ensure a free domain name with any hosting purchase. They make money through affiliate sales – anytime someone makes a purchase through the third party domain dealers or web hosts, the app is credited and receives a portion of the sale.

**HELPFUL WEBSITES**

1) Appy Pie (www.appypie.com)

Appy Pie is the largest no-code app development platform out there. They have a DIY software you can utilize that includes features like a loyalty program, push notifications and step-by-step navigation. Plans start at $18/month.

2) AppMachine (www.appmachine.com)

AppMachine allows you to create an app based off the content already available on your website. They have35 pre-coded building blocks you can assemble to your liking. You can make your own apps or become a reseller and build apps for others.

3) Game Salad (www.gamesalad.com)

Want to make a game? Game Salad has a creator function that allows you to put together 2D games through a drag and drop method. It was originally formed for educators but is open to everyone and requires no coding experience. They have a free or a premium version and publish to all major app stores.

4) BiznessApps (www.biznessapps.com)

BiznessApps is targeted towards small business owners and communities. They have mobile ordering, reviews and direct messaging as features. If you build apps, you can also resell them on this platform.

5) Sell My App (www.sellmyapp.com)

Got this developing thing down and ready to start flipping apps? Consider listing on SellMyApp. You earn 90% commission. You can also use this site to shop for premade app templates.

**DOWNSIDE:**

You have to constantly be updating the app and fixing bugs. The market is heavily saturated so your app needs to do somethings others don't. Even then, you'll find that getting the word out and bringing users to your app can be a struggle.

**YOU KNOW YOU MADE IT WHEN:**

You have an app that's a Worldwide phenomenon, Pokémon Go style. You've has millions of downloads and make money from advertisements and upsells. You keep a team of designers on hand to troubleshoot but generally you take the final program that was paid for and created once and sell if over and over again as long as there's a demand for it.

# CHAPTER FIVE

# *Existing Assets*

*"Do what you can, with what you have, where you are." - Theodore Roosevelt*

### Strategy No. 22: Rent Your Property

If you have a home, car, large appliance or other item that people would want to use for a limited time only, you can consider renting your property for a profit. If it's space and/or items that you're not using, this is a great way to make something from nothing.

**PAY RATE:**

If you're renting your home out, the price you make will vary depending on your location, the amount of space you're offering and the level of amenities therein. On average, the daily rate for an AirBnB rental is $160. You can charge cleaning costs to the guest and take a security deposit in case of damages.

If you're renting your car out you can expect to make a minimum of $35/day. Those with high end equipment like cameras, drones and camping gear can make anywhere from $20-$200/day.

**WHO IT'S SUITED FOR:**

You are someone who doesn't fuss over personal space. You share easily and are trusting. You don't mind lending your belongings to others and taking a risk that they won't be returned in the same condition. If you're looking to host others versus just loaning your things, you should be welcoming, easy to talk to and warm.

**SUCCESS STORIES:**

Jenna Kutcher and her husband Drew run two AirBnB rentals in Hawaii – The Kutcher Condo 1.0 and The Kutcher Condo 2.0. They rent for $215/night and typically sell out a year in advance. That means that, conservatively speaking, they're netting at least $1k/month in rental revenue per condo when you factor in the costs to maintain/pay for the units and their properties are paying for themselves.

**HELPFUL WEBSITES**

1) AirBnB (www.airbnb.com)

AirBnB is the most popular site for short-term rental properties. You'll be hard pressed to find someone who's never used it at this point. If you're looking to put a room or home up for rent, you can find steady bookings here provided you price yourself within the market. It's also easy to reach SuperHost status if you get good reviews, allowing you to earn more income and be featured prominently in search results.

2) VRBO (www.vrbo.com)

VRBO is an alternative to AirBnB and is often used by people seeking longer stays. If you're a host, you want to maximize your visibility and list your place on both.

3) Turo (www.turo.com)

Turo is a car sharing marketplace where guests can rent cars from local hosts across the US, Canada, the UK and Germany. Turo checks and validates each driver and car owner before they can rent from the marketplace. The car owner sets the car's price, location and information. The average owner makes $600/month.

4) Peerspace (www.peerspace.com)

Peerspace is an online marketplace that connects photographers, event planners, entrepreneurs and creatives to event, meeting and production spaces. It's like AirBnB but for professional purposes. If you have an office, studio or commercial space, you can rent out all or parts of it when you're not using it.

5) Curb Flip (www.curbflip.com)

Do you have a driveway, boat slip, empty lot or designated parking spot you're not using? Post it on CurbFlip. You'll make premium rates if you live near a stadium or somewhere you can offer monthly parking at a bargain, like New York City. This is a great option for anyone not comfortable opening up their home on short-term rental sites and wanting to keep distance between renter generally. No money changes hands in person, it's all done online. Note: if you're in the UK, try Just Park for the same concept.

**DOWNSIDE:**

When you're renting out your things, you always run the risk that they will get damaged. People can be careless with belongings that are not their own. Make sure you screen any users thoroughly and charge a security deposit if you're able. Most of these platforms favor the user when it comes to disputes, not the host, so protect yourself accordingly.

**YOU KNOW YOU MADE IT WHEN:**

You have a top ranked listing on a respected site. You sell out all available dates the moment you open them and are comfortable with the amount you're charging. You are covered should any damage occur and are in the position to turn away bookings from clients with bad or no reviews. You make steady earnings every month and in the case of real estate, make more than enough from rentals to cover your monthly mortgage and still turn a profit.

## Strategy No. 23: Sell Your Photos

Selling photos online can be a lucrative career path. If you have a big library of photos you've taken over the years, you can sell them individually as stock photos or prints. If you have photography skills, you could also sell your photo services for travel or engagement photoshoots in destinations around the world. You don't need to have a physical studio space or fancy gallery exhibit to be a real photographer. The online world is ready to soak up your gifts.

Note that while platforms like Instagram are great for growing brand awareness and establishing a following, they're not your business model. Use these platforms to promote your photography products or services in some other way and funnel your fans towards a purchase or booking. You deserve to get paid for your work.

**PAY RATE:**

If you're selling stock photos, you won't make big bucks. Typically, photos sell for less than a dollar each and you still have to payout the third party platforms that are hosting your photographs and showing them to potential buyers. If you go wide, open up accounts with at least 4 different stock photo websites and add 5-10 new images per week, you can earn around $200-$400/month.

Consider submitting your photos to competitions to gain more recognition and merit a higher fee as a result. You can also pitch photo essays to newspapers and magazines. BBC publishes these more than any other type of content and pays approximately $400 for a photo essay of 8-12 photos plus captions.

If you open your own photography company and offer photoshoots plus editing services, your income level jumps exponentially. Event photographers charge $150-$250 per hour with a 2-hour minimum, while a wedding photographer charges $1,000-$3,000 flat for 6 hours. This doesn't take into account earnings made from prints purchased after the shoot.

## WHO IT'S SUITED FOR:

You're someone with a photographer's eye. You don't need prior experience or fancy equipment – all of that will come as you grow and learn. You're creative and have an eye for detail. You're patient, flexible and have good people skills. You can make your subjects feel at ease and bring their personalities to life in photographs.

## SUCCESS STORIES:

Helena Carmouze had no idea when her husband bought her a DSLR that it would be the beginning of a successful small business. Nine years later she runs Provoke Photography, an award-winning, home-based photo studio that's been featured on outlets like Wedding Wire. If you want to hear more about Helena's journey, make sure you tune in to the Work from Home Diaries podcast, episode 3.

## HELPFUL WEBSITES

1) GettyImages (www.gettyimages.com)

This is one of the world's largest online image marketplaces. By having your content on here, it'll get in front of big marketers and companies. You have no control over the purchase price but it might be hundreds of dollars and of that, you get 20%. Note that Getty Images demands exclusivity so any photos you post on there cannot be listed elsewhere.

2) Adobe Stock (www.adobestock.com)

If you're already an Adobe Creative Cloud user, selling your photos on Adobe Stock should be a seamless transition. It's integrated with all your other apps so you can drag and drop an image from Lightroom or Photoshop into Adobe Stock. You can earn anywhere from $.50 to $5 per sale of a photo. You also have some unique features here, like the ability to edit the details of your photo after submission to add relevant keywords. They also have a responsive and on-call customer service team.

3) Flytographer (www.flytographer.com)

Flytographer started as a way to capture proposals abroad and has grown into a general travel photography services provider that employs freelance photographers around the world.They do all the work for you; you just show up and deliver the pictures. You need two years of experience and conversational English to apply.

4) Local Grapher (www.localgrapher.com)

Local Grapher is a similar concept to Flytographer, only in addition to photo shoots they offer video shoots, photo tours and photography workshops. You need 3 years of experience to apply.

5) Zazzle (www.zazzle.com)

Zazzle allows you to sell products with your photos on them, from pillows to t-shirts. This could be a fun alternative to offering prints after a shoot, especially for themed events like bachelorette parties.

**DOWNSIDE:**

To make a living on stock photo websites you'd need to upload hundreds of photos. At times, the prices for photos can be low and it can be months between sales. If you're breaking out on your own, you have to consider the cost of framing and shipping if you're offering physical prints. You also need to have high-end camera equipment with crisp, clear photos to market yourself as a professional. You can't be hired to photograph a wedding and show up with your iPhone for the job.

**YOU KNOW YOU MADE IT WHEN:**

You can take photos and enjoy your craft while still making a good living from it. People appreciate your aesthetic and are eager to support you by buying prints, commissioning work and leaving you glowing reviews. You set your own schedule and choose how often you want to have a photoshoot or travel for a campaign. You have a library of tens of thousands of photos you've taken over the years that bring you passive income and are often picked up for advertisements and promotional materials.

## Strategy No. 24: Sell Clothing and Accessories

They say one man's trash is another man's treasure and nowhere does this hold true as much as it does with clothing. There are entire vintage shops dedicated to fashion and accessories – all the other old stuff gets lumped under the umbrella category of "antique store."

Fashion is cyclical so what's hiding in the back of your closet today may come back into style tomorrow. This means that if you own clothes, especially designer labels that you've kept in good condition, you could be sitting on a goldmine.

Many people progress from selling their own used clothes online to opening an e-commerce store once they see it's possible to turn a profit. The difference between the two is that most e-commerce stores specialize in new clothing, whereas this category focuses on resale. Also, by selling on apps and resale companies, there are minimum barriers to entry. Anyone looking to make extra money can start completely free of charge, without having to pay for shipping, arrange a payment portal or develop a website.

**PAY RATE:**

How much you make depends on the quality and rarity of the clothing you're selling. If you have a ballgown or Michael Kohrs suit, they'll fetch more on resale than your baseball cap or American Apparel t-shirt.

Generally, buyers are looking for a deal. If you're selling everyday items from your own inventory, you can make between $200-$500/month. If you have a storefront through an app like Etsy and decide to supplement your own collection with vintage finds or new pieces, you can make upwards of $5,000/month.

**WHO IT'S SUITED FOR:**

You are someone who has always invested in quality pieces. You take good care of your clothing, bags and shows so that they look like new years later. You like to declutter and make room for new things. You don't have an emotional attachment to clothes and can part with them without regretting it later.

**SUCCESS STORIES:**

Natalie Gomez left her job as a merchandise planner at Macy's and started selling clothes online that she found in her closet. When her first dress sold for $40, she quickly cleared out all of her inventory and started buying and flipping clothes from retailers like Abercrombie or Zara and vintage stores around New York. Her Poshmark store has grown to almost 300,000 followers and she's branched out and opened an ecommerce store called Costume Baldor, earning more than $10,000 a month in sales.

**HELPFUL WEBSITES**

    1) ThredUp (www.thredup.com)

Touted as the world's largest online thrift store, ThredUp is the place to go if you're doing one mass cleaning out of your closet and want to do the least work possible. You put everything in a bag, mail it to them and they get back to you with a quote. This isn't the most lucrative of the resale options, but it's one of the quickest since you don't need to wait for a buyer.

    2) Poshmark (www.poshmark.com)

Poshmark is an app that allows you to post clothing and accessories for sale. You set the price and Poshmark takes 20% commission. They provide pre-paid labels and USPS priority boxes are included for free. This app acts like a social network so the more people you engage with, the more views your shop will get.

3) ASOS Marketplace (www.marketplace.asos.com)

ASOS is an option for Europe and UK residents. You pay a £20 monthly membership fee and can cosign your used items alongside independent brands and boutiques from around the world. You must have a minimum of 10 garments in your store at all times and can earn up to 80% commission.

4) Etsy (www.etsy.com)

For a long time, Etsy was regarded as a place for crafts and custom items. Over recent years it has evolved to include used clothing. If you have something unique that you can't find a home for elsewhere, the catch-all nature of the Etsy marketplace might just be your solution.

5) The Real Real (www.therealreal.com)

This site only works with high-end brands like Prada, Chanel, Marc Jacobs and Louis Vitton. You can make between 55% to 70% of the sale price depending on how much you sell with them each year. They do everything for you, including arranging pick-up, paying for shipping, authenticating, photographing, pricing and selling your items.

**DOWNSIDE:**

You may not always get the price you think your items deserve. If you get emotionally attached to clothes, you could be offended at lowball offers and have a hard time letting go of items. You also need to be sure your items are in pristine condition to get good reviews and future customers.

**YOU KNOW YOU MADE IT WHEN:**

Your clothes pay for themselves. You always have the newest labels and fashions and after you wear something twice, you sell it for almost full retail value. You're a fashionista so people follow your store and trust your style. You're highly ranked and because of your clout, you get approached with free clothing or affiliate links for major brands.

## Strategy No. 25: Offer Professional Services

Already have a job you like and just trying to find a way to take it online? It's easier than you think.

If you have a job where you offer professional services and spend the majority of your day in front of a computer, chances are you could break out on your own and do the job from home or a coworking space.

**PAY RATE:**

Your rate at home can mirror whatever you would charge in the office. Whether it's per hour or per project, you don't have to take a fee cut because you've remote. You're still providing the same quality of services.

If you used to charge $400 to prepare tax returns while working for a brick and mortar company like H&R Block, charge the same or more when you break out on your own. If you got paid $30/hour to do marriage counseling in an office, charge the same to conduct virtual sessions.

**WHO IT'S SUITED FOR:**

You don't like the day-to-day of office dynamics. You resent having to put your lunch in the company fridge and being unsure if it will be there when you get back. You're tired of entertaining office politics. You waste a lot of time at the office chatting or browsing the internet because you're checked out or uninvested and feel you'd be more productive on your own.

**SUCCESS STORIES:**

Jaime Lieberman of Hashtag Legal is an attorney that specializes in providing legal services to online entrepreneurs. She works on cases involving trademarks, copyrights, business entity formation and more. The best part? She is location independent and doesn't waste funds paying for a costly office space every month.

**HELPFUL WEBSITES**

1) 8x8 (www.8x8.com)

This is a free video conference platform, much like Zoom, only it doesn't have a 45-minute time limit. There are features like captions, recording and the ability to host up to 50 participants.

2) KeySearch (www.keysearch.co)

If you're going to target customers in paid marketing efforts, it's wise to know what search terms they're looking for. KeySearch is a keyword research tool that provides comprehensive data about the topics you want to write about, including an estimated number of searches per month, a competition score that tells you how difficult it will be to rank on page 1 of Google and suggestions for alternative words to target.

3) Interact (www.tryinteract.com)

Looking for a way to attract new clients? Interact is an online quiz maker that you can use as a fun lead magnet that entices readers to sign up for your email list to get their full results. You can make the quiz work in your field. If you're talking about money management, for instance, you can make a quiz about how financially savvy a person is. This tactic works because people are always curious to learn more about themselves.

4) Trello (www.trello.com)

If you need to get a team organized in one place, you need a project management system. Trello allows you to assign and delegate tasks, share notes and files and work on projects together. It's a primarily free service that lets you work with an unlimited number of boards, lists and cards.

5) Loom (www.loom.com)

When you're onboarding a new team member, it's important to train them so they know what you expect. Loom is a free screen and video recording tool that you can use to record training videos on your laptop. They automatically process and save all recordings to your digital library.

**DOWNSIDE:**

It can be challenging to move your business online. Many people aren't as productive at home as they are in an office. You'll also lose a sense of comradery that comes with seeing coworkers every day. It can also be difficult to attract and meet with clients when you don't have a traditional office setting.

**YOU KNOW YOU MADE IT WHEN:**

Your remote work income surpasses your full-time income from your past life in corporate. You're happier and most satisfied than you were sitting in a cubicle waiting for time to pass. You're energized about your field again and can't wait to start working on new projects and ideas.

# BONUS

# *Work from Home Diaries Podcast*

*"Every new beginning comes from some other beginning's end." – Semisonic*

Woo hoo, you made it! I hope you're absolutely buzzing with ideas about how you can turn your talents and assets into an online business.

If you're looking for a sign to take the leap, I have big news for you -- This. Is. It. Don't wait a second longer! Whether you're looking for a side hustle or whole new career, you are capable.

To help you get started, I put together an interview series with people I know personally who make a full-time living online. In these 7 episodes, you'll learn about how to make money in several different roles, from influencer to freelancer.

Here is your login information:

**Link:** www.jenonajetplane.com/workfromhomediaries

**Password:** homeiswheretheworkis

A disclaimer – this series was originally recorded on Zoom and was going to be presented as videos. I wasn't happy with the quality of the recordings so I decided to repurpose the audio into a podcast.

Now, I could've tossed the project altogether and let perfectionism stop me from taking action but I follow my own pillars of success! So, while it's not perfect, this podcast series is done and it's the first step towards what I hope will be an ongoing show on Apple podcasts.

I hope that after reading this book, you finally see all the different ways you can make money online and take action. After all, the world (wide web) is your oyster.

# *About the Author*

Jen Ruiz is a lawyer turned travel blogger and writer. In 2017, Jen set out to take 12 trips in 12 months while employed full-time as an attorney. She surpassed her goal, completing 20 trips in 12 months to destinations like Greece, Iceland, Cuba, Thailand, Italy and Argentina.

In 2018, Jen transitioned to working remotely full-time. One year later, she surpassed her full-time attorney income with remote work earnings. She is a #1 Amazon bestseller, Readers' Favorite Award winner and was named Top 40 Under 40 by the Naples Herald

Jen is also a two-time TEDx speaker and winner of two North American Travel Journalist Association awards. Her story has been featured by The Washington Post, Huffington Post and ABC News.

Jen shares tips on how to obtain financial and location independence on her website, www.jenonajetplane.com. She is active on TikTok, Facebook, Twitter, Instagram and Pinterest. Reach out and follow along!

If you found this book helpful, let others know by leaving a review on Amazon. Your support will help spread the word about work from home opportunities.

Made in United States
North Haven, CT
26 May 2023